I WENT, I SAW, I ATE

I WENT, I SAW, I ATE

(OVERSEAS, OVERWHELMED & OVERFED)

BERNICE ZAKIN

Copyright © 2012 by Bernice Zakin.

Library of Congress Control Number:		2012909839
ISBN:	Hardcover	978-1-4771-2193-1
	Softcover	978-1-4771-2192-4
	Ebook	978-1-4771-2194-8

All rights reserved. No part of this book may be reproduced or transmitted in any form or by any means, electronic or mechanical, including photocopying, recording, or by any information storage and retrieval system, without permission in writing from the copyright owner.

This is a work of fiction. Names, characters, places and incidents either are the product of the author's imagination or are used fictitiously, and any resemblance to any actual persons, living or dead, events, or locales is entirely coincidental.

This book was printed in the United States of America.

To order additional copies of this book, contact:
Xlibris Corporation
1-888-795-4274
www.Xlibris.com
Orders@Xlibris.com

Table Of Contents

1964

September 29th-October 1st New York to Lisbon, Portugal 15-21
October 2nd-3rd Madrid/Toledo 21-26
October 4th-6th Madrid 26-33
October 6th-10th Mallorca to Paris 33-39
October 10th-14th Paris 39-49
October 14th Return Home 49

1966

September 20th New York to London, England 51-52
September 21st-24th London 52-57
September 24th London to Paris 57
September 25th-28th Versailles and Paris 59
September 28th-30th Venice 60-64
October 1st-2nd Florence 64-67
October 3rd-4th Montecatini/Pisa 68-72
October 4th-5th Florence 68-73
October 6th-10th Rome 73-73
October 10th Return Home 83

1967

November 5th New York to Athens, Greece 85
November 6th-9th Athens 86-94
November 9th-13th Jerusalem 94-108
November 13th-16th Tel Aviv 108-113

November 16th-18th Haifa 113-118
November 19th Return Home 119

1968

October 7th New York to Como, Italy 123
October 8th-11th Lake Como To Valenza 124-128
October 11th Lake Cuomo to Lugano & Milan 128-129
October 12th-13th Milan To Rome 129-131
October 14th Rome to Florence 131
October 14th-18th Florence 132-135
October 18th-21st Nice 136-141
October 22nd Beaulieu 142
October 23rd Return Home 142

1976

October 19th-20th New York to Monte Carlo 144-145
October 21st-22nd Monte Carlo/Nice 145-149
October 23rd San Remo 149-150
October 24th Cannes 150-152
October 25th-27th Nice 152-155
October 27th Return Home 155

1977

October 19th-20th New York to Palermo, Italy 156-158
October 21st Palermo/Monreale 158-160
October 22nd Agrigento 160-162
October 23rd Cantania 163
October 24th-26th Taormina 165-172
October 27th Tormé Norman 172-175
October 28th Return Home 174

1978

November 4th-12th New York to Paris, France 176-189
November 12th Return Home 189

1979

May 14th-20th New York to London, England 192-198
May 20th-23rd London 199-204
May 23rd Amsterdam 202
May 24th Amsterdam to Copenhagen 204
May 24th-28th Copenhagen 205-209
May 29th Return Home 210

1979

October 4th-10th New York to Paris, France 212-220
October 10th-13th Amsterdam 221-226
October 13th-17th London 226-232
October 18th Return Home 233

1982

October 2nd New York to Morocco 234-235
October 3rd-5th Casablanca/Morocco 236-238
October 6th-7th Rabat 239-241
October 8th Medina 245-247
October 9th Fez 247-248
October 10th Mohamedia 248-249
October 11th-13th Monte Carlo 249-250
October 13th Nice 251
October 14th San Remo 252
October 15th-17th Monte Carlo 253
October 17th Return Home 253

1983

October 29th New York to Tokyo, Japan 254
October 30th-November 2nd Tokyo 258
November 3rd-6th Hong Kong 258-259
November 7th Aberdeen 263-264
November 8th Return Home 264

Dedication

(A repeat from previous books but always relevant)
Always to the memory of my late husband Albert Zakin
To my children Nancy and Jeff, and Barbie and Ken
All my grandchildren: Lizzie and Jon, Carly and Peter, Andy and Dana, David and Susan, Kenny and Alyson and Debbie and Michael
Finally my great grandchildren: 13 in number and they are not to be slighted, but are too numerous to name individually (I do know their names however!)

ACKNOWLEDGMENT

Very special thank you to Elise Alarimo, for helping me all the way through and Xlibris for printing everything so well.

TRAVEL BOUND

The following experiences were a most exciting part of our lives and we were extremely grateful for the opportunity to go to all of these wonderful places. We had a terrific time on each trip and we hope that whoever reads the following pages will enjoy revisiting them with us.

September 29, 1964
NY to Lisbon Portugal

Left New York on TWA - rainy weather and ready for this big adventure

Arrived Portugal 9/30/64—gorgeous weather

At long last we were at the airport for our first trip abroad and feeling slightly nervous. Shirley and Eddie were with us for dinner which we had at Eastern Airlines. We bid our farewell to them and then got on the plane at TWA.

A rather mixed group was awaiting the flight—children—a few older ladies, several couples and some business men.

Our seats were #11. but unfortunately poor Al's seat was slightly broken and it would not recline. However it turned out rather well for him, as after a bit of futile tinkering during the flight by the steward, he was offered first class accommodations—leaving me behind—oh well it was his birthday and he deserved it.

I had an interesting conversation with the man next to me. He was quite philosophical but we both found no solution to world dilemmas. We had a lengthy discussion about the personality traits of people in other lands in relation to our own, which was an unusual conversation especially on an airplane.

Our dinner was fair—just nibbles and then the movie (Tom Jones) was shown. I took a pill and settled down for a nap and Al was apparently very comfortable up front.

It seemed like no time at all and we then sighted land—Lisbon time 8:30 to 9:00 AM and I felt quite like Columbus. This was an exciting experience so far and everything looked so orderly from the air.

An unusual clock made of grass in a mound with numerals (Roman) all around, was sighted on the ground and then whoosh—we landed. Al came back to the poor man's land in the plane's rear and glowed with the aftermath of a champagne and caviar feast plus a comfortable seat. What a birthday present!

We then took a taxi to the Ritz Hotel where we were fortunate to obtain reservations thereby cancelling the one we had at the Hotel Embaxada. We unexpectedly met Dorothy Solar and L.D. Cohen in the lobby then went to our room which had a magnificent bathroom—dual sinks, marble walls, heated towel racks, separate shower, bidet, a round toilet seat and everything was very comfortable, plus the beds had huge pillows.

After a much needed nap, we went down to have lunch for which we were too late but the Cook tour man suggested a little "snack bar" called "Pisca Pisca" which we could not find. However a young student understood enough of my French and was able to direct us. In fact, he accompanied us which was very accommodating. He was a student at L'Ecole Speciale, a supposedly fine school for exceptional pupils.

"Pisca Pisca" was quite small and quaint. We ordered a delicious parsley omelet and pineapple with white port wine over it. This was truly Nectar of the Gods and ambrosia to say the least, and Al was given a shoe shine while we ate lunch which was a most unusual feature in a restaurant.

Then we went back to the hotel where we acquired a guide, Fernandez, for a tour of the city. This was quite interesting—the wealthy residential area was magnificent and the "Alfama", which was the poor section had narrow winding and cobbled streets. There was just enough room for one car, and it had steep hills and was crowded with people who appeared poor but were content and happy. In fact, everything we saw seemed clean despite of the living conditions.

There were a lot of fish on display in little stalls in the area, and it was malodorous but picturesque. We also took pictures of a few landmarks overlooking the city on the hills and then we went to the "Stufa Fria" in King Edward Park. There we saw a most unusual greenhouse—quiet and restful with music playing (there was an open concert hall at one end). It had completely planned foliage with little brooks, rippling water falls and natural stone steps unusually arranged leading up in an irregular lane to the top. There were little grottos within which romantic young people sat in loving quietude on stone seats, and were really just extensions from the wall. There were also beautiful pigeons with white fanlike tails abounding, swans were on the lake outside and it was a lovely sight indeed.

Then we went off to the shopping area where I purchased a few gifts at a ceramic shop and finally went back to the hotel bar for beer and delicious salted almonds.

Both Al and I got dressed and went down to the Ritz dining room to have dinner in the most beautiful room. We ordered sliced salmon from a board (wooden and long with a carved fish face and tail), had langouste soup and brochette of lamb, tea and "faisca" wine—a rosé—excellent. Great cookies were served in a spun sugar basket—lovely, lovely, lovely!

Off to "Faia" a fado restaurant where the entertainment was most exciting. Talented singers sang a few plaintive songs accompanied by guitarists (their feet were resting on tiny stools). The master of ceremonies also sang, joked and danced a few native dances which was certainly fun and different. Then we returned to our room for much needed sleep—Goodnight!

October 1st—Lisbon—Cloudy

We had a leisurely breakfast and were served continental rolls individually wrapped in paper plus wonderful jams and sugar cubes in red paper covers (all very pretty) and had good tea as well. Al was still sleeping so I went downstairs to the shopping area in the hotel and purchased a few souvenirs, where I met Irene Schaeffer just coming in from New York, so this apparently seemed to be a 5 towns meeting place.

Then we took off for the day's excursion. First we went to a castle and Fernando, who was our guide, and was a pleasant Portuguese with a Jewish grandfather—(Leopold Cohen) took us to the palace of Queleuz, which is still used for visiting notables, Eisenhower, Grace Kelly of Monaco, Queen Elizabeth, etc. It had beautiful rooms, floors, tiles and gardens and was quite grand indeed.

Next we went on to Sintra—a quaint little town with a palace up on a hill overlooking the town square. It had magnificent tiled walls—a huge kitchen with a long spit and a chimney area four floors high. (There certainly must have been much feasting in the days of yore). We then purchased a few gifts at the Bazaar Central—a little nearby tourist shop. Finally we were off again and drove on a quite densely shrubbed and wooded road. It was glorious, but truly like mountain climbing and in fact it was almost like a fairy tale pathway. We stopped at a little park or garden that belonged to one of the kings—it was called "the garden of Camillias" and was beautiful with lovely white swans swimming gracefully in the little lake, just like a secret garden.

Pïna Palace was next—high on a hill about 500 feet above sea level and which was a fantastic structure that took 72 years to build, with moats, draw bridges, patios, courtyards and turrets. It was a huge castle to outdo all other castles and the view from one of the courtyards was absolutely breathtaking. You could practically see all of Portugal below which was truly remarkable.

On to Estoril, which was a disappointment except when we visited the country club and watched a club member tee off and take a "mulligan", also the Palace hotel was pretty but not exciting. The town itself was small and fairly commonplace however a new hotel is being built by Jewish builders. It will be called "The Estoril Sol" and it should be quite grand.

We visited a tiny hotel next. (Almost like a pension), in Caisçais where there seemed to be a waiting list of 4 months for reservations. It was called "The Albatross" and was lovely and charming with a view of the ocean through a telescope. This was a glorious and exciting thing to see.

Then we went back to Lisbon via the ocean road which was reminiscent of the road from Miami to Palm Beach along the ocean. Our dinner was not too pleasant however and we could not go to "Avis" as we had to meet the Solars and the L.D. Cohens. They took us to "Tavares", which was mediocre, although my lobster was good what there was of it. Oh yes—I forgot—we had lunch at Seitais—a castle converted for tourism—it was a pleasant lunch and had a wonderful atmosphere and delicious pastry.

After dinner we went to a bull fight which I enjoyed although Al did not. He found it to be cruel although it was exciting and quite humorous at times. They do not kill the bulls there, not like in Spain.

We then returned to "Pisca Pisca" for that delicious pineapple in port wine which was really great, then off to bed after a weary day.

Friday, October 1st—Lisbon—Weather Lovely

We had a good night's sleep and awoke to the usual continental breakfast which was very good.

After we went downstairs we bumped into the Schaeffers. I think they were a little confused about their plans. Then we went off to Avis and visited a little art gallery where I purchased a small water color. They also had some lovely pottery but it would have been too expensive to ship it home. We then went back to the main street to a little snack bar for tea and rolls and great biscuits filled with shrimp, and we found it to be extremely European and delicious. After that we went upstairs to settle our effects and were off to the airport. Madrid here we come!

Understandably we hated to leave Lisbon, it was really so enjoyable. Although the Iberian airport proved to be most confusing. It makes one feel inadequate and foreign. A nice gesture however was a gift bottle of port wine—compliments of the government. Then we got on board and had a nice flight.

Sunday, October 3rd—Arrived in Madrid

We arrived at the Hilton only to find that our room was not ready. After a little dispute we finally landed in an inferior room and definitely a flea bag type of quarters. There was no hook in the bathroom, and it was a tiny room and unpleasant so far.

After a little nap we went to Los Pablos—a bar down the street, where we drank a "fino" and then went to "La Puerta De Moros" a restaurant in an old castle or mansion belonging to a Duke. The whole place was quite attractive in a dilapidated sort of way. Our dinner was gazpacho, chicken in champagne sauce and a sweet cake for dessert, which had strawberry, whipped cream, chocolate and custard, and everything in the dinner was quite good.

We then returned to the Hotel Palace for a look-see and also visited The Ritz which was more elegant, and where the old world charm was quite apparent. However we couldn't get reservations at either one, so we were stuck at our hotel.

After we taxied back to our flea bag quarters at the Hilton, laundry time became a necessity. Thankfully our inflatable hangars were a real joy, but our bathroom now resembled a family wash day. It certainly wasn't an adequate bathroom.

Our guide José Grandela met us at 10 o'clock in the lobby and he was most charming and quite a continental gentleman. Then we were off to the Royal Palace for the experience of a lifetime—3000 rooms of which we saw magnificent examples of luxurious craftsmanship in an extremely extravagant manner.

The porcelain room was breathtaking and the Chinese room had embroidered silk walls and matching upholstery on the furniture. This was where they performed the royal baptisms. We also saw the wonderful platinum chandeliers. In fact the chandeliers and ceilings in all the rooms—were so hard to describe. The oohs and ahs poured out of both of us. We still can't believe we were seeing such magnificence.

Then we went to Retiro Park and had a lovely ride en route. It was quite like Central Park in spots, and the lake with boats was very picturesque. The University was grand in scope and the buildings were all new and constructed on an old revolutionary site.

These buildings were all quite far apart and each nationality was housed separately in the various dorms. It was rather austere and not at all like the campus life as we know it in the United States.

Next came the Prado which had wonderful paintings by Goya, Velasquez, El Greco and Murillo. The most well known Velasquez masterpiece was viewed in a separate room, through a mirror—almost three dimensional, and the Goya sketches were marvelous, almost like cartoons of the time. They were quite biting in tone, but complimentary and satirical as well.

We understand that El Greco used models from mental institutions to attain a facial "Lost" quality. He used elongated body structure for unreal people and normal structure for real people. The tapestry pathway in the Royal Palace was fantastic by the way.

We subsequently went to La Baraca for lunch—a typical restaurant in the peasant manner where we had delicious paella, gazpacho and fish soup. It was a decorative place and quite hard to describe.

Then we walked along San José Antonio and had our picture taken on the street so I guess we looked like real tourists which we really were.

We then returned to the hotel to keep Al's business appointment with a young Spanish Jeweler who had his cousin with him to help interpret. We all managed to converse easily but they had nothing of interest for Al to buy.

Unfortunately Horsher cancelled our dinner reservation—rather cheeky I must say. So we went to La Commadore instead. This was a lovely place—very clean and modern and we had sliced Salmon (Nova Scotia) with chopped eggs—(yellow and white), parsley, onions, and lemon wrapped in cheese cloth. I also had lobster which I could not eat completely as it made me nauseous all day and I hoped I wouldn't throw up.

Happily we met the Lerman's an older couple (Jewish) from San Francisco who were on a world tour for 6 months. They were at the next table and we became friendly so they came with us to La Zambra—a flamenco club. We could hardly find the place and our poor driver was bewildered and unable to move the car which finally stalled on a curve of a hill. It was quite a deserted area too, so it was a bit frightening.

We finally did reach La Zambra and it was the greatest. There was national folk dancing—primarily the clapping of hands to a marvelous vibrant beat and the dancers were using castanets as well. Each person in the group danced separately, then sat in a circle with 3 guitarists in the middle. It was colorful and exciting with the crackling sound of the clapping—very hard to describe.

The star was a beautiful Castilian. She had a perfect profile almost like Dolores Del Reo and was dressed in a red and black polka dot costume, long and beruffled. Her hands were so graceful, almost like swans' necks. I think her name was Marie Helene. Al was entranced and didn't want to leave and I didn't blame him.

Then we went back to our hotel with the Lermans, who were staying there too and so to bed. My upset stomach was not better and I was still nauseous—oh well I guess I had the Spanish stomach!

Sunday—Toledo—Weather beautiful

Poor Al awoke this AM with my complaint (only worse). I didn't know if he would be able to make the trip to Toledo. I felt like a heel to go alone but he insisted.

I finally left without him and sat next to a girl from Washington, D.C., who was originally from Vancouver and she was quite enjoyable and pleasant to be with. Toledo was the most remarkable place, old world entirely, like going back in time. There were cobblestones which were hard on the feet and our tour guide was difficult to follow. It was congested there as well because they had too many tours booked on Sundays. The sword factory was a disappointment but the city itself was unusual. The cathedral I would be unable to describe even in my wildest dreams. The ornate decorations really can't be believed, especially when you realize everything was man made. It was just as if I had arrived in a fairy tale. It was absolutely huge and it took 300 years to complete so it was really remarkable that such architectural ability existed in those early years.

The carvings, statuary and paintings plus the ceilings of the Muresco type are only found in Spain. The jeweled treasures, the Cellini plates, the globes of the different continents, the jeweled tower encrusted with emeralds, rubies and sapphires all set in gold, the beautiful gates covered with silver, the coral pieces, the priest's vestiments and robes of petit point, and the gold, silver and velvet embroidery including the laces, were all too beautiful to be real.

The masterpieces in the chapel choir room with organs on either side and carved figures on 3 levels were just fantastic. The "window" in the cathedral was like a carved painted skylight and unbelievable. No appropriate accolades were possible to describe such magnificence.

The room with the cardinals' paintings and the Muresco ceiling was almost like a mosaic work of wood and gold leaf—wow!!

Then we went to El Greco's home which was charming and old. There were beautiful paintings, old furnishings and a lovely garden. Our next visit was to the synagogue where only one wall was remaining, with the original decorations like a lacework of stone. The seats had dark mahogany on the sides only, the synagogue was on 2 levels and open in the center. It became a church after the Inquisition, and the ceiling of cedar wood was from Lebanon, and was brought especially for the synagogue.

At last we saw El Greco's masterpiece displayed in a very guarded manner. It was behind an iron gate and when they drew a curtain like on a stage, the light was then turned on and behold! A magnificent piece of work. The colors and faces were so alive and realistic, you could almost touch them.

The guided tour was most unsatisfactory—it was too rushed and I couldn't even buy postcards and I almost got lost several times in the winding, twisted streets. However, it was a remarkable day. I felt so awful that Al missed it—to come this far and miss such a tremendous sight was more than a disappointment. It was a disaster!

Finally, I went back to the bus and the return trip was uneventful. The "plains of Spain" were wide and far reaching and the color of the earth was pinky beige, like clay. The mountains in the distance were quite visible and olive groves were frequently seen in passing.

Al was still ill and I hoped it would soon pass, thankfully however he slept all day, so I wrote some postcards but needed many more. Thank heavens though Al seemed to recover sufficiently to have a light dinner therefore we canceled the Jockey Club and went to Casa Botin, which was regional and small. It was quite crowded, like an Italian restaurant in the 40's in New York. It had tile walls and the old décor dated way back with the history of Hemingway's interjection in the "Sun Also Rises"

It was great that Al was able to have dinner, and in addition we had a pleasant waiter who understood my Spanish. I had pessado soup (like bouillabaisse) and roast baby lamb.

We also became friendly with the couple at the next table. They were young Norwegians who spoke English very well. we spent the evening with them strolling the avenues, and then stopped into an outdoor café for tea and coffee.

They were really a lovely couple and lived in a small city "Stavanga" in Norway. He was a civil engineer. They had 4 children and had lives similar to ours.

Eve (the wife) may be able to send us a ski sweater for Kenny from Norway, that would be fun and he would love to have it I am sure.

They even used the same tablets for upset stomachs that we do—"Vioforms" but television was only 2 years old in their country. They had dinner at 4 o'clock, breakfast at 8 AM and just a sandwich at lunch about 11:30—coffee perhaps at 9 PM and their college situation was just as difficult as ours.

We then returned to our hotel after an exchange of addresses and a fond farewell. It was a lovely evening—goodnight!

Still in Madrid—Monday, October 4th—

Weather lovely

Slept a bit late today and then went to the lobby where we did some gift shopping. Our next stop was Serrano Street—a lovely avenue of fine shops, and passed an unusual butcher shop. It was clean, white and all marble plus the meat was perfect. The store was a sparkling vision. We also saw a balloon lady and an old pharmacy with nothing but apothecary jars. I bought a piece of chocolate candy and a package of gazpacho soup and I hoped they'd be good. This was very modest shopping indeed!

The streets soon started crowding up with the noon day walkers and everything became quite busy. All the little sidewalk cafes filled their seats and the city took on a bustling air. We were entranced with a beautiful little baby whom we saw in her carriage and she was clean and sparkling just like in a picture advertisement.

Club 31 was our choice for lunch. This was a really delightful experience. I had my favorite gazpacho, and poached eggs with round green noodles in a cream sauce. It was marvelous and the little crepes filled with apricot jam were delicious. The waiters were wonderful and constantly hovered around us. I must say "the good life" is really great!

Then we took off to the jewelry factory which was a vibrant little place. It was extremely clean and well organized and Al bought a few silver bags to see if they would be saleable at home. They were nice people to deal with and had everything all laid out and ready for us which was most gracious.

After leaving them, we walked on San José Antonio, where we had some good cake and then went back to the hotel to write more cards and to rest.

Our dinner reservations were at Horchers an old and very well known restaurant. It was quite lovely as you entered, where there were bowls of fresh raspberries and strawberries facing the door which was most enticing to see. We had fried eggplant topped with Russian dressing. (The waiter kindly got the eggplant from a neighboring store as they had run out of it in Horchers). Then we had beef stroganoff with rice and "AMBROSIA" for dessert. This was raspberries with whipped cream and had a fantastic taste sensation. However, Al decided to have raspberry crepes. They put the raspberries in a pan with sugar, butter and white brandy and cooked them, then they added the crepes and heated them some more. The whole thing was poured over vanilla ice cream and it was utterly divine. He really loved them, who wouldn't!

I must say the service at Horchers was great. I was given a footstool for my feet and perfume was poured into the finger bowls. Trés glamour indeed!

Finally we went back to the Hilton where we met the Meltzers. We had a drink with them and so to bed.

Tuesday, October 5th

We left at 8:30 A.M. with our guide, Joseph Grandelo for La Ville de Los Cardos and El Escorial. Thankfully we had a private car and for the most part drove through a fairly barren countryside. It was quite mountainous in the distance, and then we went on to the final resting place of the revolutionary soldiers. This was a monumental construction built on the side of a huge mountain with an imposing cross 300 feet in the air. The chapel itself was rather austere but of enormous proportions and the air was so clean and dry you could almost hear everything from miles around.

Off again to El Escorial—a building at least 2 blocks long. It was over three hundred years old and it housed an amazing collection of tapestries, many designed by Goya. They were all very bright and still colorful and depicted the activities and games played by the people of that time period. It was amazing work, most artistic and a joy to behold.

We also visited the crypt below which contained the burial room of the kings, queens, princes and royal children. This was extremely regal, all marble and bronze and with quiet majesty.

The library was truly magnificent. It was a long room with all the bindings of the books facing the wrong way, so that only the gold pages showed. This supposedly made the books easy to maintain for long periods of time.

In the center were the most valuable volumes encased in glass cases. What creations they were! The drawings and script were truly works of art.

We then drove back to Madrid and to Club 31 again for lunch. This time we had lobster bisque, coquille St. Jacques which was baked in a pastry shell, (not a real one) and a raspberry soufflé for dessert. It was a bit too rich but Joseph ate with us and related many interesting tidbits about the local customs and notables. So time passed quickly and enjoyably.

An interesting event occurred when the Minister of Commerce came to the restaurant while we were there and was pointed out to us.

We also met the Meltzers there too. They had spent the entire morning buying paintings which was smart of them, as the art here is great,

Finally we went back to our room for the final moments of packing and also to take a farewell peek at Madrid. A wonderfully alive, busy city which was metropolitan in every sense.

Tuesday, October 6th—Mallorca

The flight to Mallorca was uneventful and the weather was lovely but the airport at Madrid (this section) was small and no one spoke English and it made us feel like sheep being led to slaughter. We took a caravelle which is a French plane—it was very quiet and we soon arrived at Mallorca which had a busy airport full of stalls and people. Just like Penn station at Long Island (only worse). There we were met by a Hotel employee who whisked our luggage out quickly and then drove us the 20 minute ride to Son Vida. This was really a most beautiful hotel high on a mountain, and furnished exquisitely—but the manager could only confirm our reservation for 2 days. We hoped we'd be able to stay longer anyway. Al was still sick unfortunately and our room was small even though it was attractive. A black and white linen scenic mural was behind the bed, there were white walls, an aqua ceiling and stone blue spreads of heavy linen with draperies to match, all of which made it quite beautiful.

Met the Schaeffer's there and the Schleins. We had dinner with Lynne and Bob and another couple (the Schucks, Sam and Lucille). We ate outdoors while a good orchestra played, and during dinner a German guest got up and sang some gay and happy songs, which was quite a bit of fun although we were thoroughly exhausted and so to bed.

Just received a letter that the Port wedding was subject to change. Buddy disappeared! Al was also still not well. We had breakfast on our terrace facing a mountain, then went downstairs to the pool and gardens—a magnificent sight. We saw gorgeous foliage and the setting was like a sparkling jewel in the sun.

Sat with the Carltons—(Marian and Phil) friends of Irene and Manny and also they were cousins of Miriam Gordon. They were sweet people and gave us some pills for Al which I hoped would be effective. Then we had lunch on the terrace with the Schleins and the Schucks, and had gazpacho and melon which were quite good.

Off again to Palma where the stores were really a madhouse. There were so many per square inch that it was possible to go wild trying to get our bearings. Lynne then took me to Bonet where I bought some hankies, really gorgeous and I also bought an exquisite cloth. It had beautiful embroidery all blue and white. Al and Bob met us there and we walked around for a while and then I bought a linen mat set, which was quite lovely.

The suede things were also attractive and all the little odds and ends were so different and exciting to see—it was quite a place in general.

We then returned to the hotel after a short stop at the bar, which led to a general cocktail hour with the Schaeffers and Schleins. We also went up to Irene's suite which had a fantastic series of rooms too amazing to describe and afterwards we had our usual nap and dressed for dinner.

Another cocktail hour with the Schleins, Schucks and a couple from New York was next on the list. We seemed to be drinking quite a bit! But were not tipsy.

Finally about 11 o'clock, we left for El Patio, supposedly the best restaurant in Palma! The food there was perfectly dreadful and the service was slow. However we enjoyed the evening as we met some nice people from Johannesburg South Africa. This was really the most wonderful part of traveling. One of the women was from New York originally but had been living in Paris for 35 years. She's a translation secretary. But when we got back to the hotel we found a cable—The Port wedding was off! How horrible for all of them!

Thursday, October 8th—Cloudy—Mallorca

The morning was a little windy, cloudy and mixed with sun and after our breakfast on the terrace we had a call from the desk. They will let us stay through tomorrow. We now have one more day to sweat it out and be able to stay longer. I went to the beauty salon in the A.M. and the operator did a fairly nice job, however the wind started blowing and to my misfortune, the woman in charge would not sell me a hat in the gift shop as it was reserved for someone else.

Nevertheless as I was blowing about at the pool, I met the new owner of the hat and she sold it to me which was absolutely kind of her. People are really so nice in Europe.

We then had a lovely lunch with Lynne and Bobby on the terrace, and it was much more pleasant being with just 4 people.

Once again we had our usual rest period and I was able to reorganize the luggage, after which we went back downtown to Palma for more shopping although we did not buy anything. However we soon went back to the hotel for cocktails again with the Schleins. Unfortunately a calamity occurred after we returned to our room. We had a drippy shower which sprayed water into the foyer, but after it was repaired we had another cocktail hour with the Schucks, the Schleins and Rabbi Rudin and his wife. She was most interesting and quite sophisticated and clothes conscious. She also used to be a fashion coordinator and was British. I later learned she was his 3rd wife. Quite a Rabbi!

We had dinner at long last at 11 P.M. at Son Vida. I had sliced salmon which was really delicious and Al had white fish in an orange sauce served with orange slices. I must say it was an interesting combination.

Everybody got very friendly after that and then the violinists started serenading us with lovely Italian songs so it was an extremely poignant and touching evening.

We bid farewell to Lynne and Bob as they were leaving tomorrow quite early in the A.M. I promised to call her mother to say all was well, when we get home.

Friday, October 9th

We were awakened this A.M. by a surprise call from Dorothy Shankman. They were staying at the Hotel De Mar. The Meltzers were there too. We arranged to meet (the Shankmans) at Loewe's at 11:30 A.M which we did, and her husband was a pleasant guy and seemed to hit it off well with Al.

We then went to a leather place she knew "Saiga" and wound up spending the morning there and we both bought pony skin coats and hats. They really seemed to have such attractive clothing in Majorca. We also bought an emerald green knit and suede outfit for Nancy and the values and styles were great. The best we had seen in all the stores in the area.

After a busy morning we chose Anthony's for lunch. All of us had bouillabaisse then went back to the De Mar to see Dot's Hotel. The view there of the Mediterranean was fantastic and the water was bright blue—with rock formations jutting out into the water in little coves. There were beautiful flowers—geraniums, and petunias all around. It was really lovely. The hotel was quite modern and the Meltzer's suite was fantastic with a huge black marble bathroom the size of our living room. Really something. Then we went back to our hotel to rest before dinner. It was now 5:30 P.M.

Cocktail time was about 9:30 P.M. and we discovered there was a banquet scheduled this evening for all the notables of different countries in the tourism association. Each table setting had 5 glasses for wine, and it was very impressive I must say, but they served no hors d'oeuvres except nuts and those wonderful little olives stuffed with anchovies.

Sadly the lobby was all disassembled to accommodate the big party, so the Meltzers and the Shankmans whom we had invited to have dinner with us, could not really see our hotel at its best.

However we still had a lovely evening. Dinner was smoked salmon, their special steak was served for all, and then we had fruit. Poor Mario, the head waiter was unable to properly take care of everyone and he was quite upset. He was expecting to go to New York to work at "21" in a few months and I hoped we'd be able to see him there.

Before we knew it, it was 1 o'clock and we bid our farewells. We went up to the room to find that my coat had arrived. It was really lovely. I imagined Nancy would like it too. Off to sleep and tomorrow we were leaving. Oh yes—we bought a little water color in the lobby last night. The usual tourist type—but nice.

Saturday, October 10th—Mallorca

The weather seemed cooler and breezy, but sunny. We had breakfast and went off to town to get the sales slip for my coat. Then we wandered around the shops a bit and finally went back to Son Vida for lunch, where we had gazpacho and sardines. Finally we packed our suitcases and then just sat around. There was not much sun so we left for the airport which was busy but not as bad as when we arrived in Palma.

We then boarded the plane and met a Frenchman on the flight who had been at Son Vida. He was head of the Hotel Association and said he would help us if we called him for any reason. He was extremely nice and it was a gracious gesture for him to make.

Saturday, October 10th—Paris (Cold 48 Degrees Fahrenheit)

The plane trip was great. It was a French caravel and there was no vibration whatsoever. We had a nice dinner with some kind of cold fish, delicious asparagus, olives and tomato salad, cold chicken and artichoke hearts, champagne, cheese and then cake.

But the French people rushed onto the plane so quickly there was no room for Al and I to sit together. So the pilot was accommodating and put us in First Class, (it looks like that's where we belong!)

After landing in Paris, we had a nice taxi driver who pointed out various places of interest to us, Les Invalides, Napoleon's tomb, a tour of the Eiffel Tower, the Obelisk, The Arc de Triomphe, and the Champs Elyseés. It was really an impressive sight to enter Paris for the first time as the streets were slightly wet because it had rained for 3 days and therefore everything glistened, the lights twinkled and the fountains played its spray upon the water. We also saw the Seine and the direction of the Left Bank.

We soon arrived at the Claridge Hotel which was an old relic located on the Champs Elysée. Our room was a horror. No shower! Just a tub and it was so deep it looked like a pool. Maybe we can change tomorrow but at present, all the other rooms were occupied.

However we unpacked and went out walking and it was simply terrific to be in the Paris streets. The clothes in the shops were so attractive and displayed interestingly. No mannequins were used. The clothes were just strewn on the floors of the store windows and were quite different looking.

We stopped into a little grill place and had eggs and chocolate. Then we walked some more and finally went back to the fleabag—what a room! Who said it doesn't matter where you stay? I found 2 letters from Nancy and they were very sweet. Then off to bed with hopes that it would be a nice day tomorrow. A good thing I had a warm coat, it was necessary. Brrrr!

Sunday, October 11th—Paris

We were awakened at 8:00 A.M. by one of Al's French trade people. It was so early—oh dear! He will meet us here at 5:30 today.

We went back to sleep till 9:00 A.M. and were awakened again by Alan Golboro—what a surprise! I didn't think we'd know anyone in Paris. We are meeting them for dinner this evening. We finally decided to get up and to have breakfast. The usual croissants and rolls, etc. They were delicious and were served with good current jelly. The cups they brought us were extra large—quite different from the doll sized cups we had in Madrid.

We got downstairs about 10:45 A.M. and hired a taxi to drive us around Paris and we were so fortunate that our driver was a young Parisian who was most accommodating and who understood my faltering French, and believe it or not I understood him.

We got along famously and at all the places of interest, he stopped so we could take pictures. Paris was so exciting!

About this time it started to rain so we decided to have lunch. Our guide suggested the place where he had lunch everyday

"Au Pied de Cochon". The place was completely filled but with our driver's influence, they set-up a tiny table for us on the 3rd floor. This was a completely middle class family kind of place on Sundays, with a dancing type of waiter who flitted about the tables at break neck speed. It was amazing to watch his maneuvers. We then had the most wonderful onion soup gratineé. It was a deep bowl completely sealed with cheese, gummy and crusty with a huge slice of bread and onions inside. Delish!! Al had a wonderful trout with almonds and I had hors d'oeuvres. Al also had a raspberry melba with divine toasted almond slivers and it really was a marvelous lunch for both of us.

We then passed all the public buildings and for the most part they were beautiful. We also saw the famous churches such as Saint Chapelle with the statue of the Saint on top, then Notre Dame, a magnificent structure with turrets and gargoyles, and Sacre Coeur, which we entered and listened to a bit of the service. From there, was the most fantastic view of Paris. The location was way on top of a hill and the vista below was widespread and breathtaking. Sacre Coeur by the way was in Montmartre, a most exciting place. All the new artists gathered there to paint and sell their paintings. A surprising number of which were quite good.

Cute little cafés were all around and while we were there we saw an exposition of old (antiquated) motor cars and fire engines that they displayed for the purpose of deciding which car could go the slowest!

We also went to the Eiffel tower and walked under it. This was really an amazing structure, it was a lacework of iron, and we also saw the gardens of the Tuilleries which were beautifully laid out and carefully planned.

After lunch our driver took us to the Louvre where we parted, but he had truly made the morning a worth while expedition.

At the Louvre we found out that guides were not available on Sundays so we ventured forth ourselves to find what we wanted to see.

We found the "Mona Lisa" first, she really had an amazing expression, and it is true that from every angle her eyes follow you. We then saw what we thought was a copy of the "Last Supper", a wonder of wonders.

Happily we accidentally found The "Venus de Milo". This was really a thrill. I practically touched her and they had fragments of her arms in a glass case nearby. We also saw a sphinx almost intact, and the room with the Medici murals was quite interesting, but in general the buildings themselves were amazing! I never knew the enormity of the Louvre. It was a series of buildings that were huge and impressive.

Wearily we taxied back to the hotel where we arranged to change rooms. We now have a smaller room but with a stall shower (no curtain).

Mr. Landin, a man with whom Al does some business in New York, arrived promptly at 5:30 and spent about 45 minutes with us. A Frenchman with a Jewish accent is really incongruous, then after he left we showered and dressed for dinner.

We arranged to call for the Golboros and it really was fun to see them in the middle of Paris so off we went to Tour D'Argent, a very expensive restaurant, but supposedly a necessary tourist trap. It was a beautiful place high up over the Seine. We all ordered melon, a kind we never saw before. It was round with a slice on top arranged like a pot cover. Then we had Caneton (duck) which was pressed in front of us in rather a stagey setting. This was served with potatoes soufflé with empty spaces inside and crisp outside. The duck was served with the liquid from the pressing on top of it. Then they gave us slices of the crisp duck, and a salad with a wonderfully subtle dressing.

Alan ordered profiteroles and they served him 3 huge ones with chocolate sauce, but the rest of us had raspberries, sugared and served with whipped cream—mervailleuse! During dessert time there was the pièce de résistance. The restaurant overlooks Notre Dame and on Sunday nights the church is lit up at a specific time and in different sections. They then turned off the lights in the restaurant so it was possible to see the church completely and a more thrilling experience cannot be found.

At the end of the display, fireworks were sent up—really a tremendously exciting spectacle.

After dinner we all went to "The Lido", which was actually quite different from The Lido at Long Beach. This was an extravaganza barring none. There were beautiful showgirls á la Ziegfeld and as I said "barely bosomed and bosomly bared". They wore gorgeous costumes and then there were scenic effects of increasing splendor, plus excellent entertainment, including an ice skating show, a prestidigitator, a ventriloquist and girls who juggled tables on their feet. There were also acrobats who stood head on head with just a ball between them.

Next there was a water fall scene with a practically nude dance team and at the end, the nude man disappeared into the water. A crazy orchestra with very funny musical effects came next and the finale was a bejeweled, befurred, bare bosomed, light flashing, fireworks kind of sensation. Truly an amazing performance, and although it was touristy, it was worth seeing because of its perfection of styling and production.

Thank heavens we finally made it back to the hotel where we were happy to call it a day.

Monday, October 12th Paris—Cool

I awakened about 8:30 A.M. but Al slept till 10:00 A.M. We left the hotel around 11:00 A.M. and went to Laurentis, the tie factory. We had great difficulty finding the street as it was so tiny (Rué St. Joseph), but we ordered 2 dozen ties and Mme Laurentis recommended "Chez Jean" to us for lunch, and she especially touted the bouillabaisse and the Portuguese white wine.

While we were eating we struck up a conversation with the people (the Steinbergs) at the next table. They were from a small town near Luxemburg and were Jewish. Al conversed half in Jewish and English and I in French and English. It was such fun. They were in Paris to buy raincoats and toys for their shops so we went with them to a wholesale raincoat place, and Al and I bought beautiful raincoats, and also one for Nancy—light blue silk. There were so lovely to us—truly unbelievable, as the French are not known to be friendly to Americans. Mrs. Steinberg said that at Hanukah she would send me a clip to attach my handbag to the table as I had admired her clip which was unusual.

We then went all over the wholesale fur district with them and to a cloak and suit house, the owner of which was in a prison camp with Mr. Steinberg during the war I even tried on a few coats just for fun but there was nothing I wanted to buy. At any rate it was a great day and we managed to understand one another quite well.

We finally went back to the hotel and had a much needed rest and then we called for the Golboros and went to Berkley for a really marvelous dinner. I had oysters and artichokes hollandaise, roast duck with wild mushrooms,(tiny little things) and then raspberries for dessert. I really love them in Paris. Al had black current sherbet for his dessert, and Alan had orange sherbet in an orange, and lemon sherbet in a lemon. They were served together and looked wonderful. Betty Jane had terrific sweet breads and rice that we all tasted—yum yum. We also had gorgeous fresh figs and the waiter finally brought us all manner of other choice fruits.

We fruitlessly tried to get into "New Jimmys" but we were not allowed to enter as it is a private club and we did not have entry cards—too bad! So we walked around a bit instead (all around montparnesse).

We then took a taxi to the Hotel Continental—a lovely old world high ceilinged affair, and walked on the Rue de la Paix for a while, and then had tea at the Café de la Paix.

Finally went back to our hotel and have decided to stay in Paris for two more days. We loved it and didn't want to leave!

Tuesday, October 13th—Cool And Pleasant

Tried to arrange for a flight to New York on Friday, but alas everything was booked so we must leave Thursday at 1 P.M.

Unfortunately we will lose a precious day. However we went to look at jewelry shops and saw some lovely pieces, mostly in the Place Vendôme. Then went to Michael Swisse for perfume and now that kind of gift shopping is behind us.

After that we went to one of Al's jewelers where they spoke no English so I had to interpret. It was a fun experience and they thought I did quite well. By this time it was 3:00 P.M. and we were starved so we went to a little grill for a cheese omelet.

We also stopped at Sagil where I tried to purchase a handbag, but they had nothing I liked however they were getting some others for us to see tomorrow.

Finally we went back to our Hotel as we were both rather weary and ready for a nap and a shower. Picked up the Golboros at 8:45 P.M. and went to "Moutin De Panurge" where the rolls were shaped liked penises and they had finger bowls shaped like chamber pots filled with rose petals. The dessert was shaped like a penis too and a young lamb ate the crumbs off the table. Everything there was Rabelaisian and funny. It was a tourist place, but cute. Betty Jane ordered a musical trout (they put a music box on the table) and they also take pictures of the girls with garters around their thighs. It was silly but fun.

We then all drove up to Montmontre to see the Moulin Rouge and the Place Pigalle which was a little too seedy for us what with all the nude shows and dregsy looking characters, so we taxied back to the Continental. En route we saw prostitutes in an alley, and then saw 3 girls running like mad away from the police. They were soliciting in the wrong area and were afraid their papers would be taken away (according to the taxi driver). It was quite interesting to see them fleeing like rabbits. They were nice appearing too.

Had a drink at the Continental with Betty Jane and Alan and then returned to our hotel. The ties that we ordered had been delivered as was the perfume in a lovely airlines bag. (It was quite a nice way to carry it). Sadly we had just one more day left in Paris and practically not a blank page left in this book.

By the way, we saw a rather downtrodden weedy individual in the restaurant who became quite a bit friendly. Al gave him his card and he then asked Al if he was Jewish. When Al said yes, he squeezed Al's hand and said he was also, but motioned not to let his friends (with whom he was sitting) know about his religion. He then said "goodbye Albert". Al was quite touched by the encounter—it was strange how being Jewish all over the world is like being part of a brotherhood. It was truly an amazing and quite wonderful experience.

Wednesday, October 14th

This morning we went to the jeweler's office and had difficulty finding him, but we finally made it after questioning several people. Finally the little old concierge told us where it was. She was a typical concierge in a crowded little room with dogs, cats and an old man with a long beard. Really weird. Al completed his business and off we went to Sagil where I ordered a bag. The crocodile ones were really gorgeous but cost $140, so I bought a lizard one instead. Then we went back to the Montmontre and we tried to eat at " A La Bonneé Fourchette", but it was closed, so we landed at La Mère Catherine that was a real tourist trap.

Needless to say we were quite displeased. Then we wandered around the square where we bought 2 paintings and hoped they would look good at home. But they only cost $20 each a most inexpensive amount.

Rain suddenly started to come down so we stopped at a Boulangerie for a pastry that was delish and finally we taxied back to the hotel.

After depositing our bundles in the room we took a farewell walk on the Champs Elyseés which was most pleasant. Then since we had 2 reservations for dinner, we had to make a decision which one to choose between "Cris de Paris" and "Elyseé Matignon".

Oops—choose the wrong one. "Elyseé Matignon", and the food was just so so. It was really just a neighborhood type of restaurant, although the people dining there were all nice looking and well dressed. However, it was not an elegant dinner.

Since it was still raining, we taxied over to the George V—another disappointment. Not at all what I would like. No old world flavor at all. We did meet the Lerman's however, from San Francisco in the lobby. They were the couple we met in Madrid. Poor things, they were quite lonesome and they have 4 more months to go to complete their world trip.

We then said farewell to the Golboros and went back to our hotel to pack and to contemplate our departure.

This was really a wonderful vacation, never to be forgotten and perhaps hopefully to be repeated again some day. Au revoir Paris!

1966 LONDON
Tuesday September 20th

Mother awakened—nervous and excited and announced it was 5 to 6, time to rise to prepare for flight time at 10. I do believe she was up all night in expectation of the trip.

Everything was fine at the airport—Shirley drove us in a light rain and Aunt Min was already there and quite calm,

We had the wide space in row 14 (oh dear my unlucky number) the "three girls" sat together and Al was cozily ensconced behind us with an empty seat between him and a quiet Chinese man.

It was a lovely flight and the "girls" behaved remarkably well—particularly because they were kept busy eating a fairly dull lunch, going to the ladies room and with Mother opening and reopening her purse checking its various contents.

At last we saw the "lights" of London town and down we came in a smooth landing.

For an interminable distance we lugged our totes and coats and happily trudged to our waiting limousine which was a welcome sight. There was about a 20 minute drive to the Grosvenor House through the outskirts of suburban London and over the "Fly Over Bridge"!

Thankfully we had lovely rooms—modern heated towel racks in the bathroom and capacious closets with built in accessories.

We all went out for a walk and had a slight snack at a coffee shop near the Dorchester, where we had scrambled eggs and yummy toast (butter was in a small crock). Then to bed and had a good night's sleep.

The last time I noticed, the clock said ten past 2 PM—our time in New York was about 9PM but we were very sleepy nonetheless.

Wednesday, September 21st

Al and I got up at 7 A.M.—showered, dressed and called the "girls" at 9. Then all of us met downstairs for a light breakfast and we were all off to see the changing of the guards. It was colorful but not too impressive. The only exciting moment was when the troops entered the gate—a large crowd was gathered snapping pictures and kept in line by Bobbys on beautiful horses.

We finally went back to the hotel where we engaged a guide for a tour of the city, where we saw Big Ben, the Parliament, 10 Downing Street, etc. and also stopped at the Tate Gallery and saw the Turner exhibit, however ours was better in New York.

All of us had an inferior lunch in a restaurant next to Fortnum and Mason and then returned to the hotel to rest. Then we dressed for dinner and the theatre.

Our dinner reservations were at Scotts—a very good fish restaurant. Dinner consisted of crab in avocado and fish filet with shrimp, lobster and mushroom sauce. I ordered tea, but wonder of wonders—they don't have tea in that restaurant for dinner. Can this be England?

Off to the theatre and saw "The Killing of Sister George" a play about lesbians and radio serials. It was amusing and pathetic—both. It is supposed to open in New York, but I think it will be too sophisticated for New Yorkers. However there was a wonderful performance by Margaret Leighton. The theatre was tiny but lovely. We then tried to go to the "Ivy" a supposedly fine restaurant, but they had no room for us so we finally landed at a nondescript place called "The Drumstick For Ten".

My tummy was still a bit queasy from the darn virus I had back home and I hoped it would clear up before we got to Paris as I was looking forward to some great food there.

I hate to say that London was a bit disappointing to Al—He much prefers the excitement of a more foreign flavor.

Thursday, September 22nd

Awoke at 9:30 AM, very refreshed and we walked to the Dorchester for breakfast which was an unsatisfactory affair. Then went to W. Bill where we purchased some nice sweaters for Kenny.

We had a so so lunch at Fortnum and Masons, which nevertheless was a truly wonderful place for food and shopping. They had all luxury items but our lunch was not too good. I had a mushroom omelet with a delicate watercress garnish. I also had a raspberry soda and then we were off to Liberty for scarves, etc.

While we were at Fortnum & Masons Aunt Min politely asked what they had in the basement. A very formidable and pompous appearing elevator operator said "rats madam". It was quite hilarious.

Again we went back to our hotel for a bit and then we proceeded to Lottie Lubbock's for tea, and had a most pleasant visit. Her son Jules now has a wonderful English accent and is a bright well rounded young man with a beard. He owns an interesting cubist painting by a friend of his—Erick Koch who was considerably talented, I thought.

Lottie served us wonderful Scottish salmon and Ada's favorite date cake as well as a raisin cheese cake. It was all lovely and tasty and Lottie was most charming and hospitable.

We went back to the hotel at this writing and then off again to the theatre to see "Robert and Elizabeth" a truly delightful show—gay, with pathos, very colorful and thoroughly enjoyable. We finally got to the "Ivy", which proved to be a wonderful restaurant much like Sardi's—we had marvelous steaks, then taxied home and considered it to have been a most gratifying day.

Took the usual huge black taxis to and fro and they really looked like shiny black patent leather bugs in the street especially from our bedroom windows. I did hope the weather would remain so pleasant as it makes traveling much easier.

Friday, September 23rd

Awakened at 9 and hurriedly showered and dressed and dashed down to the waiting car to take us to Windsor Castle. It was hopefully going to be an eventful day. The weather was perfect but just a little brisk in the A.M.

The approach to Windsor was lovely—the countryside was lavishly spotted with flowers, in every variety and hue. The castle itself was a huge affair built with the usual turrets and wings. We gaped avidly at the Queen's doll house, a fantastic assemblage of miniatures—each piece perfect with every room complete and then we went through all the state rooms with the aid of a walkie talkie.

We also saw a few well known masterpieces of Holbein and a Rembrandt's self portrait and one of his mother, and on the way to Windsor we were able to see Hogarth's home. The town of Windsor itself was perfectly charming with winding little streets lined with antique shops and appealing tea rooms. We even saw Nell Gwynn's home which was now an antique shop—It was a typical old English village as we had always imagined it.

Then we proceeded to Christopher Wren's home where we had a lovely luncheon, soup, leg of lamb, very good potatoes rolled in parsley and apparently cooked in chicken broth, braised celery, spinach and a fine salad. We then had tea on the terrace which overlooked the Thames—it was a most wonderful spot to spend a few days away from the hubbub of London and fun to see the boats along the river.

We returned to our hotel by way of Eton College where we saw several school boys in their striped pants and tailcoats, stiff collars and ties. They really looked impressive, not at all like the American rather sloppy attired students.

Our driver was a lovely person—Donald, who took us back to the hotel where we had a little tea and again wearily went to our rooms, for a good night's sleep.

Today Al and I went to Temple. A disappointing Yom Kippur affair—quite different from our service at home, although the Rabbi was a fine gentleman who welcomed us and invited us to come back tomorrow.

Then we were off to the Connaught. Again, it was disappointing. It was quite old, decrepit and small. However, we went to Claridge's next—a fine dignified hotel and it would be nice to stay there. We had dinner at the Angus Steak House nearby and then to bed.

Saturday, September 24th

Harrods was our first stop in the AM and we bought some inconsequential things and then went to Claridges where we had a delicious lunch. It was truly a lovely place. Tried to go to the little shop nearby but they closed at 1 pm so I left a note for them to send me the scale I liked.

Again we went back to our hotel and found a message from the storekeeper at Claridges asking us to return. She was a lovely person and I bought the little scale.

Then we returned to our hotel (Grosvenor House) for tea and Bobby Altman came by to visit. We then left for the airport and proceeded on to Paris where we arrived after a pleasant flight.

PARIS

Saturday, September 24th

Still the most beautiful place I've ever seen—Oh how I Love Paris!

The Hotel Crillion really was very pleasant and we found the most unexpected note from Ada Belford who was staying there. As we were a little hungry we decided to go around the corner for a bite to eat at a very cute little café then went to bed for a good night's rest.

Sunday, September 25th

We left for Versailles early in the morning for an all day trip and first we saw the Castle and then had a wonderful lunch at Coq Hardi. This was a fantastic restaurant with beautiful gardens all terraced. Of course we had too much food, which incidentally was presented magnificently. The waiters marched around with trays of fat white asparagus and they were really enormous ones, plus there were also other great items on the trays. Several of the customers (ladies) had tiny poodles in their laps, which was apparently a common sight in Paris. We also went to Au Pied de Cochon for dinner and the onion soup was still great—then we drove back to the hotel.

Monday, September 26th

A smart move on our part was when we decided to take mother and Aunt Min to board a bus tour on Cityrama, as we thought this would be a great idea for them and then Al and I wandered around the shops by ourselves. First we went to Sagil, and then to Trausseles for flowers, and on the way we also bought Nancy some lovely lingerie and a dress for myself. The next stop was to Charles Jourdan for shoes where they were beautiful and cheap.

Again we went back to our hotel and met Aunt Min and mother for cocktails at the Ritz and then returned once again to the hotel, where we rested and then met the Belfords for dinner at Gerry Gallant's suggested restaurant "Le Cris de Paris". It was slightly overrated but was a charming spot anyway although the food was not good, so we took our relatives home and went to "Crazy Horse" with the Belfords. This was a real dive, and

I was tired too. It was a strip tease joint and the cab drivers tried to overcharge us on the way out. This outing was a real mistake so hopefully we will know better next time.

Tuesday, September 27th

In the morning I went to a jeweler's with Al and then we opted for lunch and had an omelet and pastry across the street. It was divine! The mocha éclair was terrific as well!

We did a little more shopping for scarves and I think I spoke French very well. I'm quite proud of myself as everyone understood me,

We then returned to our hotel to organize our luggage and then went to The Lido with mother and Aunt Min for dinner and the show. Our dinner there was good and the show was as wonderful as the last time we saw it. It was just a marvelous production no matter how often anyone goes.

Paris at Versailles

By the way when we went to Versailles the Hall of Mirrors was beautiful to see, as well as the desk upon which the Versailles Treaty was signed and it was really a thrill to be so close to it.

We also stood on the spot where Marie Antoinette pleaded with the crowd to disperse. History becomes a vivid realization on such a trip as this and one finds oneself being completely transported to another time, peopled with all the familiar characters of yesteryear.

Wednesday September 28th Paris and Venice

Early in the morning I went with Al to the Place Vendôme and took several pictures of the gorgeous jewelry that we saw with hopes that they would come out well. Then we walked back to the hotel and took a cab to Orly airport. It was so sad to leave Paris and we had high hopes it wouldn't be our last visit.

Arrived at Orly to find that the fog was very dense and no take offs were possible. So we had a bit of lunch and then thankfully found that our flight was ready and waiting.

We were off again, this time to Venice. We all had a nice lunch on the plane but we were really much too full to enjoy it completely.

When we arrived in Venice it was 4:30 pm and it was cloudy and since the hotel car did not meet us we took a cab to a motor launch pier where we got into a boat—a little awkwardly, I must say.

We soon arrived at Cipriani and it was really beautiful and elegant beyond compare. However mother was ill, she had a fever and apparently was exhausted, nervous and under a strain. I certainly hoped she would snap out of it before we leave.

After unpacking we went downstairs to dinner and had lovely fish soup and scampi which included tender shrimp and was much different from ours. Sasha Ritter kindly sent Al a birthday cake which was delicious and sweet of her. But sadly mother had to miss it.

There was a lovely woman at the next table with an accent who congratulated Al on his birthday and when we sent her some cake, she invited us to have a drink with her tomorrow night which was most gracious of her.

The man (her companion) came from Australia and I didn't know if they were married.

I then went upstairs to see mother and she seemed a little better although still hot so I went back downstairs to stay with Al for a while, but since we were both so tired we called it a night—tomorrow is another day.

Venice was just like I had always pictured it and the houses in the water were amazing, so we really have to return to this city someday!

Wednesday, September 29th—Venice

This morning everybody slept late and then we went to the Grand Canal. What a sight! Pigeons, people and shops in abundance. The most amazing conglomeration I'd ever seen, just like Coney Island, Broadway and 42nd Street and a Turkish Bazaar. Some beautiful jewelry was at Nardis—plus linens, and glasses etc. It was really quite an array and would certainly make purchasing very exciting.

We then had lunch at Harry's Bar, and had the most delicious green noodles I'd ever eaten. They were so different from ours at home therefore it was no wonder this restaurant is so famous.

Then we went back to the hotel to get Aunt Min and to see mother. She seemed to feel better, so we boated back to the Grand Canal with Aunt Min and she was overwhelmed to say the least when she saw it.

Then we returned to the Hotel to have cocktails with the Harfords, the lady from last night. She is Yugoslavian and a former singer and he is Australian. They had a beautiful suite and were entertaining a charming group of people. One person Mr. Dreicer (like Fielding) tests restaurants all over the world—he writes, books, etc. His Secretary? "Bridget" was adorable. There was also an artist from Belgrade and the most famous doctor in Yugoslavia. It was quite a collection of nice people, and we had loads of fun.

After that cocktail hour we had dinner with mother and Aunt Min and then went upstairs to write letters. Al decided to go to the mainland but I was too tired.

Besides we expected to go back there tomorrow as the motor launch wasn't so bad. Saw the visiting Shalom there this morning, so maybe that was why the square was so crowded.

Friday, September 30th—Venice

In the morning we went to Lido, a most charming spot to see, very much like Palm Beach. We went there on a Motor Launch and passed a funeral cortege on the way which was most interesting. We also took a horse and buggy at Lido around the Island and saw the Excelsior Hotel which was a marvelous place and I would like to stay there sometime. Also saw the hotel of 4 fountains, which was extremely fine and elegant.

The beach at Lido was brown and not at all like our white sand, and definitely not particularly intriguing. Then we went back to Harry's Bar in Venice for lunch including mother and Aunt Min and also Mr. Dreicer. We again had a very good lunch—pasta, (green yum yum) lobster and raspberry sherbet. The good Italian food was really getting to me (weight wise). (How can I possibly go home and cook!)

Again we were off to Scarpo to buy some linens and then we walked around the square where we had a drink and listened to the music which included lovely well known Italian melodies.

Finally we had to go back to the Cipriani to rest and change for dinner which we had there, and again the antipasto was excellent. The chicken was tough though but we had delicious zucchini and green pasta and lemon sherbet for dessert.

Then Al and I went to the Grand Canal to the see the Gritti Palace Hotel which was really out of the way and not nearly as nice as the Cipriani so I'm happy we made the right choice. (Thanks to the recommendation by Jerry Grosbardt).

But of all things we unexpectedly met Rita and Harold Lipton and another couple Ed and Betty Meyers in the street. He was a public relations man. Rita then showed me a picture of her daughter Peggy who is gorgeous! She's the lead in a TV show coming next month "The Mod Squad" a Walt Disney production and she is currently married to Quincy Jones.

They look very well and Rita just had a very successful art show. Unfortunately however we missed going to the Guggenheim museum and did not get to see the Max Ernst show—oh well. Maybe we will come here again. I hope so. I really loved Venice.

Saturday, October 1st—Venice, Florence

We left the Hotel Cipriani quite sadly. It was truly delightful. We then took the water taxi to the railroad and the water traffic was heavy. Then we got on a beautiful train and found we were not sitting together. Our seatmates were an Italian couple from Palermo who didn't speak a word of English but we had a pleasant time together anyway as each of us tried each other's language a little bit and the woman intimated that she would send me a Christmas card which was kind of her.

We got off the train at Firenze and managed to gather our luggage together and get to the hotel taxi—it was actually a small bus which we really needed as we had loads of suitcases, what with all our purchases etc.

The hotel Villa Medici was most disappointing. The bathrooms were beautiful but the rooms were cubicles. Al raised a fuss but it may not help. I went to the beauty parlor which was inferior and quite dirty. In fact the place seemed backward compared to New York salons.

Then we took a trip to the Ponte Vecchio. What a mad house that was. Just like a Bazaar. A myriad of jewelry shops were on either side and they only had 47th street type of pieces with just a few nice ones. There was lots of coral and enamel but so much to see it made me dizzy.

We finally went back to the hotel to dress and have dinner. Sabatini's was the choice and I originally thought it was a poor one. I had minestrone soup and chicken with chopped ham and cheese (pollo Sabatini) and a divine dessert—shaved chocolate, whipped cream and a glazed éclair with spun sugar all put together. Gorgeous and delish so I changed my mind about it being a poor choice.

After walking around for about an hour, we then visited the Excelsior which was a great hotel. We tried to change but it was impossible. They were all booked so we were stuck back at our hotel to sleep.

Sunday, October 2nd Florence

Again we slept late and then went for a little walk before meeting Rita Storch and her friend Sally Shelton (we also bumped into Harold and Jean Kaufman in the lobby of our hotel).

We met Rita and her friend who was charming, and then sat in The Loggia a while near the pool, which was lovely indeed. We then went to the roof garden for lunch and that was delicious. We had tortellini (little pasta rings filled with veal and covered with a cream sauce and cheese), then we also had veal scaloppini which was wonderful with tomatoes, pimento, peas, mushrooms and white wine. Our dessert was a rich chocolate custard cake. Everything was yum yum! Oh this food!

The view was beautiful and the Capa di Monte salt cellars on the lavender tablecloths with the dull gold velvet chairs against the wood paneling in the sun was terrific. We ultimately bought the salt cellars.

Thank heavens we were finally able to change our rooms, and proceeded to do so while the "girls" waited. We now had a nicer arrangement and a gorgeous bathroom, huge wall closets, and charming sconces in an arched dressing room area.

Then we took a taxi to the Duomo with the girls (Rita and Sally), mother and Aunt Min, where we saw Donnetelo's statue and some babies being baptized in the baptistry. There was a gorgeous mosaic ceiling and Ghiberti's Bronze Doors of Paradise which were great.

The Duomo apparently was built without scaffolding on the tower, and Rita walked to the top last year. It took her 3 hours up and back. Then we went back to La Loggia Di Lanzi, which we saw last night, and also saw "Rape of the Sabine Woman", a copy of "David" and then walked past the Uffizi gallery where we had some "gelati" ice cream and said farewell to the girls on the Ponte Vecchio Bridge and then taxied back to the hotel.

After that we had a much needed nap and both of us wrote letters, and finally went to dinner at a nice place "Al Campo Doglio", where everyone was most welcoming. The people at the next table were Italian and told us to go to a particular place in Rome where our waiter spoke English, and became quite friendly, so we are sending him a Kennedy 50 cent piece as he collects coins. Had pasta and baked pear in wine for dessert and we may return here again as it was all exceptional.

After dinner we walked around town and then went back to the hotel for some tea and soon it was sleeping time. We made plans for Montecatini in the A.M. although mother and Al had a cold. I hoped they'd be alright for our next day's trip.

Monday, October 3rd Montecatini—Pisa

Left early this AM at 10:30 and visited the Villa Medici which was lived in by Victor Emanuel and prior to that, part of the Medici family. It was a wonderfully preserved castle and mostly furnished. This palace had chairs from the 14th century. Wow!

As we left, a new bride and groom came in to take pictures on the staircase. They were a lovely young couple who decorated their car with carnations scotch taped all around (very cute). After an exchange of good wishes we continued on to Monetcatini through a beautiful countryside. There were lots of vineyards, persimmon trees and family wash hanging along the way and the mountains were the Appenines and the hills of Pisa.

As last we arrived at "Montecatini" a really beautiful spa. We arrived just in time to go to one of the watering places, "Terme", which was a fabulously beautiful place, that had spacious terraces, flowers, a concert hall, and a general air of aristocratic leisure. There were also lovely shops lining the passageways in a huge courtyard.

We then had lunch at the magnificent Hotel La Pace—a gorgeous place still well occupied although the season was almost over. My Aunt Belle spent many summers there and always spoke of it in glowing terms. Now of course I understand why she did.

The town had great charm, and it was a perfect shopper's paradise. Fine and expensive clothing and gift items existed galore. We enjoyed our luncheon which was macaroni with tomatoes, zucchini, meat and cheese and peas, and then we were served grilled tiny veal chops, tender as butter, more peas and broccoli heads mixed, then parslied potatoes, salad and finally a chocolate éclair with whipped cream inside and chocolate sauce outside. Lovely cheese (the best Swiss cheese) sweet as sugar and another one like a gourmandize. Finally we had fresh peaches with an almost wild taste. (We all started to bulge after eating so extravagantly and now we have bumps throughout our bodies).

Incidentally Aunt Min had a wild tiny strawberry pie which was delicious. I tasted it to make sure it was good. (Ha Ha!)

Off again and we drove to Pisa this time. This was an amazing sight. It glistened white and sparkling in the sunlight against the blue sky and tilted at a definite angle and when you walked inside you swayed completely over. The cathedral was magnificent, huge and gorgeously decorated with gilt ceilings. (The Italians certainly knew how to decorate and embellish).

There were also many paintings and a beautiful rotunda of sculptures almost like a carousel with Lions and people depicting the life of Christ.

We then went back to Montecatini to buy Al a sweater. It was not quite what he wanted as it had no sleeves but was quite attractive and back home it will look great. (Hopefully)

Ho hum! The drive back to Florence was a weary one and we saw an accident en route but all in all it was a tiring but lovely day.

Finally when we arrived at the hotel we rested for a while, bathed and then went out for dinner. Again! Our favorite pastime!

Mother ate in her room unfortunately as her throat was bad and mine may be starting to ache.

Nevertheless we went to "Harry's Bar" but this time we walked out as it was crowded with typical Americans and we almost got claustrophobia. (are we snobs?)

So we went back to "Al Campodelia" instead and had vegetable soup—lasagna and a great big stewed peach. We also saw some huge (5 inches across) mushrooms they brought in from the market. They were dark brown and they looked like fungus plants, then we walked to the square and had tea outdoors and listened to the concert—some popular and some classical music. They played "Downtown" and called it "Chow Chow" ! Wasn't that weird?

We were finally able to get a taxi and returned to our hotel. I think I'm gradually getting a feeling of the general layout of Florence (Firenze), so I'm all set for the next visit. (I hope it will be soon)

Tuesday, October 4th

Took a "cook Tour: around the city which was a great disappointment as it covered most everything we have seen other than the Medici chapel, where most of the Medici family are buried. This had a magnificent rotunda in varying shades of marble and the sarcophagus' was topped with crowns of real jewels, rubies, sapphires, diamonds and emeralds.

The only redeeming feature of the trip was going to see the real "David" by Michelangelo" it was fantastically exquisite, perfect in every detail and a wondrous thing to view.

We then had lunch at Beppinos on the square. Here we had delicious peppers and risotto with mushrooms. Also had a gelato in the street later and then helped mother buy shoes, a handbag and gloves, etc.

I then met Al and did some shopping for the girls in his office and had a drink in the hotel bar afterwards.

My throat was still sore but I had a nap and then we went back to Beppino's for dinner. This time it was no good—I guess it is foolish to go back to a restaurant on a trip. However we were all very tired by then so we went back to the hotel and to bed. A welcome relief indeed.

Wednesday, October 5th—Florence

This day I visited The Uffizi Gallery. I was alone and had a wonderful time. I saw Botticelli's primavera, a Rembrandt self portrait, Correggio's Madonna and many other famous paintings—such as Titian's, Bronzini's etc. It was indeed a thrill. Also I went to the Palazzo Vecchio and saw many Michelangelo's and then to the Boboli gardens to see the little "fat man". He was wonderful and the gardens were beautiful.

Then Al and I went to the Pitti Palace but didn't have time to go in as we met Suzie Hillsberg for lunch and enjoyed a wonderful period of time with her at the Villa Medici Hotel roof.

She is still a sweet lovely girl and she took us to the synagogue which was magnificent. It was all in the Moorish style with a stenciled design all over the walls, painted in shades of terra cotta, rose and blue—It was huge with 3 domes and lavishly decorated. It was truly a lovely tribute to the Jewish people—more beautiful than any temple I've ever seen.

After we left Suzie we did a little more shopping and then came back to the hotel for drinks. We were completely weary but it was a perfect day.

Again we rested and bathed, then we went to the Villa Medici Hotel roof for dinner where we had Stracciatelli soup and cannelloni and then went for a little walk to the nice Manci—the bag shop. Al bought 2 shoehorns (his only purchase) but they were very attractive. Finally we went back to the hotel to pack and had to go to bed early as we were leaving for Rome tomorrow noon. It was much nicer in Florence than we expected, however I was not sorry to leave.

Thursday, October 6th—Rome

We left Florence this noon after a leisurely siesta in the hotel garden in the AM. The train was a little late and while we were waiting in the station, unexpectedly Laura Zakin's uncle came over to us and said he recognized Al. We seem to meet so many Americans that we know in Europe it is truly amazing.

Also chatted with other people at the station and almost landed on the wrong train, which required a fast rejuggling of ourselves and our luggage out of one train and into the next car of the same train. Apparently in Italy they reroute special cars of the same train.

The countryside that we passed through on the train was truly beautiful. It was a clear sunny day with the rolling hills and mountains attired in full greenery. The vineyards and little acreage farms were patterned neatly into sections, and seemingly bursting with their produce.

We luckily sat next to 2 lovely ladies from Johannesburg. A Mrs. Jaffe was one. Then we arrived in Rome after a sizeable lunch which was quite good and soon we all piled into one taxi. Our luggage was placed on the roof of the cab and I hoped it would be safe. Our fingers were crossed however.

The hotel was conveniently located but not on the Grand or Excelsior scale. Our room was rather inadequate and upon checking the rates, we thought that we might have been hoodwinked a bit. An adjustment was going to be made. (We hoped).

We then walked up the Via Veneto for a short time and had tea at Doneys which was a charming place. Then we returned to the hotel to bathe and dress for dinner. We just wanted something light after our big luncheon, so we went to Cesaria a very nice restaurant not far away where we had 3 kinds of pasta, prosciutto and figs (fresh peeled) which had a most unusual flavor, and finally baked pears for dessert, which has become our favorite.

Again we walked back to Doney's and sat outside for tea where we met a Jewish postcard salesman "Angelo". He was our first Jewish Italian. Al then went to the Excelsior dining room for a moment just to see it and met the two woman from Chicago we had met in Florence, and then of all amazing things, Mimi Weiser from Peoria spotted him and although she wasn't sure it was Al after all these years, she questioned the two Chicago women whom she knew, and then she called me on the telephone. We are having cocktails with her tomorrow evening at 8PM at the Excelsior. She is with her parents and had regards for us from Florence and Raymond Cohen in Fort Worth, whom she knew, as her daughter married a Fort Worth boy. It certainly is a small Jewish world. Anyway I had to go to bed with a bad cold and at that point hoped that I'd soon be better.

Friday, October 7th—Rome

We were all up at 7 AM and it appeared to be a dismal day with lots of clouds and completely overcast, plus the streets here were very noisy just like in Florence. Oh well, it was just our first bad day on this trip.

We met Mother and Aunt Min downstairs after breakfast in our room just in time to take a tour. We saw the Borghese gardens which were close to our hotel just outside the remains of the old Roman Wall. They were named after Aurelian from the 3rd century. We also passed the Trevi fountain which was so beautiful but couldn't stop to throw in a coin. Then we visited the pantheon which is 2 thousand years old and an architectural miracle. It was built without supports and the dome is open to receive the sun or rain as it did today. The first drainage system is still used. The Dome was originally built of earth which collapsed after the stone was applied around it, but then they built a supporting dado effect which holds the new Dome in place.

Raphael is buried there and the acoustical system was marvelous. They also played Ave Maria while we were there, in a charming and beautiful manner.

Then on we went past the Piazza Novena, a lovely square with fountains in 3 places. It is an extremely well known street with Tre Scalini an outdoor well known restaurant and several horses and buggies all situated within the square. The whole area was very picturesque.

On to the Basilica of St. Peter where we passed through a street lined with columns, to the left of which is the residence of the Pope. His window was pointed out, where he makes an appearance in Sundays for blessings. Also we saw the chimney where they send up smoke when a new pope is elected.

The interior of St. Peters was really beyond description. It had a gorgeous exquisitely decorated series of domes and arches in which there were wondrous pieces of sculpture, including the Pieta by Michelangelo which is a limp soft fluid piece of marble that seems to breathe.

The burial section of St. Peter, the first pope of Rome was gorgeous also. It was down a short flight of stairs with a marble statue kneeling in front of a golden domed altar. The center of the Basilica had a tent like structure (much like a Jewish chupah) which was designed by Bernini.

The dome itself was designed by Michelangelo and for 8 years until his death he worked on it carrying the material for its construction on little donkeys onto a small ramp way to the top and it was a most majestic sight to behold—This is the largest church in the world and surely the most beautiful.

We then went back to the hotel having passed through many other famous areas and then had a short rest until luncheon, which was a delicious affair at Tre Scalini in the Piazza Novena, where we had marvelous spaghetti with clam sauce, salad, baked peppers, and their specialty—chocolate ice cream, very dark, very hard and encrusted with chunks of chocolate candy on the outside and whipped cream on top. Will I ever get into my clothes again? No!!

Back to the hotel for a short nap until it was time to go to the beauty parlor. "Eva of Rome" which was a large place with pleasant people. Gisele did my hair—quite nicely, then mother and I bought a few trinkets—key rings etc. Again we went back to the hotel to dress for dinner.

We met Mimi Weiser at the Excelsior for cocktails. At first I didn't know her. She looked a lot older—but of course it is 23 years since we last met and heaven only knows how I looked to her. She was still a sweet girl and full of news about Forth Worth and Peoria. It was a most pleasant hour and half. Then we went to Passetta's which was quite a distance away. I guess we ordered the wrong foods although my chicken curry was pretty good. Al's veal dish was something like Kiev and he had a good wild strawberry dessert. Then we went to bed early as my cold was quite bad.

Saturday, October 8th—Rome

We left the hotel at 9:30 with our own guide, Mike De Marco who was a nice young fellow recommended by Mimi Weiser and went to the Borghese gardens where we saw a clock that works by water flowing to move the parts. It was quite intriguing and is the only one in the world. Next stop was the Spanish steps where we saw the house where Keats and Shelley lived and died. Also the Piazza Del Popolo with its twin churches and an obelisk. After that we went to the Vatican museum and the Sistine Chapel.

The Vatican is outstanding—huge and beyond description with the different halls of imposing statuary including Apollo, Hercules, etc. We also saw the torso of Belvedere that influenced Michelangelo to desire to sculpt in the same manner, and the little allegory in marble of the founding of Rome, with the girl lying in the fields and the man approaching, also the birth of the twins Romulus and Remus and then the She wolf finding the children abandoned and the place where she suckled them. The paintings by Raphael were huge murals. There was a wonderful one with Aristotle, Socrates, Sophocles, and the many others were equally amazing, and were also lavishly decorated in a continuous pattern.

The main chapel (Sistine) was magnificent with Michelangelo's ceiling telling the story of creation. It showed Adam and Eve being driven out of Paradise" etc. And of course "the Last Judgment was on one entire wall, which he completed when he was 80 odd years old. The ceiling took him 8 years lying on his back starting when he was much younger.

After an exhausting morning filled with artistic delights, we went back to the hotel to freshen up for "lunch at Pepponi's down the street and it was excellent. I had penne (Macaroni Big) with peas, cheese and thin sliced meat, salad and tea.

Off again this time to Capitalone Hill which had the oldest equestrian statue in the world.

Then we went to the Roman forum which was a group of ruins dating back before Christ. It was most wonderful to see, and of course the Colosseum where the imposing remains of the once famous amphitheatre were enough to take your breath away. It was very easy to envision gladiators and slaves being thrown to the lions.

After that we saw the real statue of "Moses" a glorious glowing piece of sculpture, probably Michelangelo's masterpiece. A remarkable sight to behold. (It was really incredible to have seen all these wondrous things).

In the morning we also visited the Olympic stadium, which is the monument (capped with gold) to Mussolini and then the arena of statues where children play ball etc. This day was the most eventful experience in all our lives.

We finally went back to Doney's and Al and I had ice cream(not too good). Then we went to buy golf gloves and ultimately to a little shoemaker to make shoes for Al. The shoemaker spoke no English but somehow we managed to speak Italian in a limited fashion.

Again we went back to the hotel to bathe and dress. Dinner was scheduled at Ranier's, an old (1824) restaurant in Via Maria De Fiore, a tiny street where even the taxi couldn't get through. It was in an old house where each room was a separate dining room. I had green lasagna, (yum yum) and prawns diavolo, pears and cheese. They grilled Mother's chicken and brought it to the table flambé and we thought the whole room would catch fire. (Thank god it did not).

Apparently celebrities came here from time to time as they displayed guest books in a glass case with well known names.

We then took a taxi back to the hotel but Al had a tough time getting one, as it was starting to rain. Then he and I went to the Café de Paris for tea.

The whole world seemed to pass by this place and I must confess I eavesdropped a bit, as an interesting foursome were at the next table. An American woman married to an Italian man with diabetes was sitting there. The other man suggested that the man with Diabetes should return to America and visit a famous Dr. E. Tolstoi who was supposedly world renowned in that field. I don't know if he ever did.

I do hope the weather clears by tomorrow as it would be nice to go to Tivoli to see the 500 fountains. In the meantime—goodnight.

Sunday, October 9th Roma

We started at 10 A.M. and went to Al's shoemaker with our taxi driver Vincent to interpret. I think the man will make Al some lovely shoes. I hope!

Then on to Tivoli where we went to Villa D'Este to see the fountains. There were hundreds of them and they were all fantastic—mother and Aunt Min didn't climb down as it meant a great deal of walking up high levels and it was really too much for them, but I'm so sorry they missed it as it was the highlight of our trip. All the water was gushing out at once from all directions in many different picturesque settings, even one coming out of a woman's bosom.

Then we went back upstairs and bought a few ceramic pieces from the market nearby, and also some delicious grapes. Oh yes, we also stopped on the way to Tivoli at a knit factory—it was a real racket to make money for the driver, but nevertheless we each bought a suit.

We then had a delightful al fresco lunch at a nearby restaurant under a magnolia tree, while a huge wedding party was inside the restaurant. We saw their lovely clean kitchen and then after eating noodles and cheese and rum meringue cake and frascati wine we visited Hadrian's villa. There we saw the ruins of his summer home with the magnificent remains of the old and calming pieces of decorated marble and also the ancient roman bath and beautiful pool etc. all dating from 125AD.

What a way these people lived ! All in all it was a most glorious day but we were happy to return to the hotel for a nap.

We straightened out our Duty items and repacked all the gifts we bought, then helped mother and Aunt Min do the same.

We decided to have dinner at Giovanni's around the corner. They had a big party so we just had a table on the street. The stracciatelli chicken was delicious. It was boned and stuffed. We had lasagna also, and then we each had a baked pear. The best one yet! (Will we ever stop eating!)

We unexpectedly met the Winston's from Palm Beach in front of "Café De Paris's and we all had good hors D'oeuvres at Harry's Bar. This included anchovy and cream cheese on toast (round) with Lee and Perrin's sauce in the middle and so to bed. Really stuffed! I mean really really!

Monday, October 10th—Rome

Awakened to find that Al was not so well, he had the usual European tummy. My cold was a little better however, so we went to the Excelsior for a taxi and met Eleanor and Johnny Seskis—we shared a taxi with them to Via Condotti and then

Al bought a borsolino hat. He really wasn't well at all so he went back to the hotel.

I then meandered around alone and bought a cloth to go with my blue dishes and also a few little purses at Gucci. Afterwards I had a lovely light lunch at Café Al Greco opposite Bulgari's and I had delicious pastry—éclairs like St. Honoré with glacé on top and whipped cream inside. I also had a small tuna fish and tomato sandwich on a tiny long roll plus an equally tiny cheese sandwich on the same type of roll. Then I had chocoletta con panna delish!

I also went to Laura Aponte and bought a lovely silver sweater then wandered around near the Spanish steps. There I sat in the sun on the ledge and then started walking up the steps to the Hassler Hotel. It was quite a trip but now I know how to get back to Via Veneto by way of Via Sistine and then turn left up the hill to the hotel Savoy, and again left to the Hotel Flora It was really quite easy. All in all I had a completely pleasant day by myself.

We all tried to go to Hostera Dell Orso but reservations were filled so we went back to Tre Scalini. It was wonderful again. I had risotto with mushrooms and chicken with tomatoes and peppers, then baked apple with prunes and St. Honoré cake. The fountains in the square were all lit up and we ate outside in a balmy breeze. Divine! Nothing quite like it in America!

If only Al felt better it would have been perfect. As we left the restaurant the waiter gave me a little souvenir shoe (ceramic) which was very kind of him. (These Italians are really charming and kind).

Then we had a wild taxi ride back to the hotel. It is amazing how my mother did not mind any of these taxi rides. At home she is so leery of fast cabs.

Well the holiday is just about over. It was a wonderful interlude which took me into a world of yesteryear and made me realize the vastness of our world and the transient period in which we live. We ourselves just walk the earth for a borrowed length of time, but the real antiquities remain for time immemorial.

At any rate, it's a wonderful—wonderful world and it was a thrilling experience to have seen these marvelous things—CIAO!

GREECE AND ISRAEL
Sunday, November 5th, 1967

Ellie and Marvin drove us to the airport for still another world adventure. This time to Athens and Israel and since it was a Temple Israel group, we knew many of the accompanying travelers.

After we had a few drinks and experienced a bit of a tizzy on the plane, due to a young man sitting in our seats because as he put it "I was just put out of my seat for wearing a yarmaka", we finally settled down to the rigors of night travel.

First we had our dinner consisting of hard boiled eggs in a vegetable mayonnaise dressing, veal chop, broccoli, potatoes, cake and cheese rolls. Then we tried to sleep and 3 hours later we awakened to the sound of a loud "good morning" in cheery tones. We also saw a beautiful sunrise but it was much too early to be up. We had eaten dinner at 11PM and now it was time for breakfast (juice and Danish) at 2:30 AM, so naturally we were all mixed up timewise.

Unexpectedly we landed at Brussels (9:30 AM their time) and wandered around the airport shopping for 2 hours but only bought some face cream.

But while we were there we noticed that the Brussels houses mostly have red clay roofs set in a patchwork setting, which was interesting indeed. Then after chatting a while with our group we got back on the plane for an unscheduled flight to Cologne.

The view of Germany (much as I dislike saying it) was magnificent. There were rolling hills with the trees all turning color and it was a myriad of reds, greens, yellows and browns. There was healthy lush foliage and a forest area as well so it was truly a sight to behold.

We then landed at Cologne for one half hour and finally flew over the Alps which were gloriously snow covered and sparkling in a pristine whiteness.

Monday, November 6th—Athens, Greece

At last we arrived in Athens and took a bus to the Hilton. It was a beautiful hotel with a lovely bathroom but we only had a studio type of bedroom. I understood that the tour would (hopefully) rotate the accommodations so we might ultimately have a better room.

After napping a bit we had dinner with the Turrels. We had quiche Lorraine, shish kebob, rice with white raisins and pignola nuts, baked tomatoes, Greek salad and pastry consisting of ground or chopped nuts rolled in honey and shredded wheat and then baked slightly. After that we strolled through the lobby and then went to bed, weary and ready to face the next day's activities in Athens.

Tuesday, November 7th—Athens

We had a wonderful night's sleep thank heavens and awakened to a beautiful, sunny clear day at 8AM. After breakfast downstairs we got on our bus for a tour of the city which included the Acropolis, Parthenon and museums, plus the changing of the guards at the palace.

The Acropolis and Parthenon were fantastic to see and there was a magnificent view of the city from the top. We also had an amusing guide and expected to go to Corinth with him tomorrow.

We also learned that the Acropolis means "a high city" and Parthenon means "the building on the temple on top". Our guide told a cute story about the American word "okay" which was originally a Greek expression "olla kola" meaning "all good". It seems that a young immigrant was tired of writing so much on packages he was paid to assess as being properly wrapped, so he abbreviated the letters to O.K.

For dinner we had red snapper soup with vegetables and Greek salad, baklava cake (no good) and fresh pears. Afterwards we walked all over town and saw many interesting things and shops, etc. Then we went back to the hotel where we bought 2 small rugs. I intended making pillows out of them. They were all needlepoint and beautiful. We also learned that the Greek key design stems from the river "Meandus", meaning "meander" which is why the design zigzags as in a "stroll".

Finally we went back to our room for a much needed nap which was a welcome period of relaxing after such a busy day.

Then we had dinner at the Hilton Hotel with the Keats's and Landis's. I had a seafood cocktail that tasted like chicken salad, sliced beef, cauliflower rosette, Greek salad and a dessert we traded (after much language confusion), for apples.

After that we went to the art gallery in the rear of the hotel, which was showing a rather wild display of geometric art, colorful if nothing else. Then we went to the "Palia Athena" a night club of supposed typical Greek origin, which had a truly great floor show divided into 2 parts. One was the classical Greek entertainment and the second half was the modern interpretation. There was one really good girl singer and an attractive young man who would certainly do well in New York.

There were also two young girls who danced and sang extremely well. They had quite clever arrangements and costumes. One of them would make a great bathing suit. It was a purple turtle neck suit with a red patent leather hip hugger skirt (very short) over it. We just had a fruit cup while we were there and got a bill for $10.00, plus we had a cleaning bill when we got back to the hotel as Al was the victim of a dropped tray all over his suit (lots of spilled food). Marcia had a sore throat so we just went there with Sam and Elaine, and Milton stayed with Marcia. That's all for today—Goodnight.

November 8th—Wednesday—Athens

This morning we were awakened by Milton Landis at 8AM to say that he and Marcia were not going on the trip today as she was still not well.

Since the hotel did not call us in time it was fortunate that Milton called us. At any rate we rushed like mad to make the 8:30 AM bus, and we even had our showers, breakfast and all, and as luck would have it, we got the last seats in the bus. Unfortunately it was quite bumpy and we were tossed around almost like a jack in the box, as we kept popping up and down. Enroute we passed the Isle of Salamus and the township or county of Attica (which is in Athens) at which point our guide Leo (Leondis) who was really very cute and personable, told us a little anecdote about his visit to America, and not knowing the language too well. It seems he was in Colorado and was trying to explain to someone that it was cold there, so he said "Colorado ice cream".

Thankfully our bus load was comprised of a happy go lucky camp like group who enjoyed singing and generally cutting up. We took the pleasant shore road with the Aegean Sea on the left and passed through Megara where all the chicken farms were located and which is the old site of the first Constantinople. The Peloponese Mountains were all around and we were able to see the town of Sparta below them. Also Leo our guide informed us that he was a Spartan as well. We then saw Kensata Beach an up and coming resort which had lovely sand and was in a Pine tree setting.

Our first stop was at Corinth to see the canal, which was actually short, probably only a mile and half long. It was originally designed by Nero but the construction itself was considered to be an impossibility for centuries. It connected the Aegean Sea and the Ionian Sea with a bridge across and was quite deep as well.

On the way back at night it was completely lit up below on each side and at that time the bridge was most exciting to see. We also had what Leo termed a stop for "coffee in and coffee out" which was a typical Israeli expression for pit stops (as Leo proclaimed).

Then we visited Mycenae to see the beehive tomb of Agememnon. This was an unusual construction dating back to the 4th Century B.C. It consisted of 2 rooms shaped like a beehive with a tremendous Lentil across the top of the door and a keystone at the very top inside which holds the whole thing together.

After that we climbed up the ruins of the walled burial grounds of Mycenae which was extremely rocky so I was grateful for rubber shoes. There was also a fantastic view passing through the old doorway with its worn grooves in the marble from old chariot wheels, and a little enclosure where dogs were kept to warn off visitors. Then we saw decorative lions on the sides of the doorway over the lentil, one on each side. The palace was above but it was so high we did not venture to it. However the sight below was truly majestic with mountains on all sides, clear and dry and with an echo resounding, and it really was fantastic to consider what we were seeing. Then we left after having some fresh orange juice, and passing through some very poor villages. There were also many tiny streets and all the townspeople were dressed in dark clothes and all the men wore suits. To us it appeared to be a rugged life as there was certainly no color in all of Greece plus the fact that they were drab people to see in general.

Our lunch however was at a charming place called the Amphytrian Hotel in Napthalian, the old capitol of Greece. It was a spotless place with delicious food and facing the Adriatic. There were also beautiful geranium bushes below with a pool and an old fort on an island, behind which is now another hotel.

We all ate moussaka, a dish reminiscent of lasagna. It was meat, zucchini, eggplant, noodles and was completely layered and then baked. Then we had lamb curry with rice and for dessert we had fresh fruit and everything was most delicious (so far we were eating like crazy).

Off again to Epidourous where the oldest Grecian clinic is situated and where the oldest physician, Episcapulous used to live. We saw the ruined friezes and columns, all with magnificent carved rosettes, acanthus leaves, scrolls and lion's heads. They were the typical Grecian designs which we still use today. Incidentally a Doric column is plain with sharp edges. An ionic column has a flat edge and is broader and has a scroll on top. The Corinthian columns have acanthus leaves on top and is the most ornate column.

The area was gorgeous, dry, clear and wooded with old trees and I believe it would really be a wonderful place for a resort hotel. Also the ruins of the old stadium were in remarkable condition with the rows of seats still standing on each side seemingly in almost perfect condition.

At last the pièce de resistance, the "Theatre" with absolutely perfect acoustical sound and we walked way up the rows of the seats. It was extremely high and our guide who was standing down below tried a few tricks. He dropped a coin on the floor of the stage, which was heard perfectly. He then tapped his chest and struck a match, and that was heard equally well where we were situated above. Then he let out a puff of breath and asked. "Do you hear me"? Someone yelled "yes I do and I smell you too". After that we wearily trudged back to the bus for the long trip home (Athens). It took three and half hours to reach there, which proved to be a most tedious ride.

Once there however we showered and then had dinner in the Taverna Nissina in the hotel. We had hors d'oeuves, roast chicken, fried zucchini, and baked tomatoes. There was lemon soufflé for dessert which they called "voulezvous". The Krieger's and Landis's joined us for dinner after which we walked to town with just the Krieger's and Morgansterns. Back in our room we organized our luggage, and being exhausted, we went to bed as we leave here tomorrow PM.

Thursday November 9th—Athens

This day we slept late and then took a taxi to the Mouriadi's shoe store in town where Al bought patent leather evening pumps, and I bought a pair of Gucci type shoes. I had to use my French, which was fun as I believe they understood me, (thank god for all those French lessons).

Then we wandered around town and went into the King George Hotel which had a rather charming old world atmosphere. We called the Landis's from there to arrange a luncheon date, and the Verby's decided to join us so we all took a taxi to Piraeous, the wharf town where "Never On Sunday" was made. This was a most picturesque harbor, thickly studded with fishing boats almost on top of each other with the town of Athens gently sloping uphill across the water in soft tones of beige, white, pale grey and camel. This was a beautiful sight, with crystal water, a blue sky, and all the fish restaurants connecting to one another.

We finally decided upon one and ordered a delicious lunch which included a shrimp dish consisting of shrimp in shells, plum tomatoes and feta cheese (lots), lemon, salt and oil served in a big casserole. It was a marvelous dish followed by broiled red snapper (we selected our own fish from the supply they had), then a Greek salad and cold, cold beer. After that we went to Zonar's for tea and dessert (ice cream puffs with custard and glacé on top). Divine! (I wondered if the natives ate like this?)

We then continued along to the handicraft shop for a few needlepoint gifts and just about made the deadline back to the hotel where a little cocktail party for us was in progress and was quite enjoyable.

Finally we departed for the airport and boarded our flight. They served a nice dinner en route which of course I couldn't eat after such a bountiful luncheon, but everyone else seemed pleased. There was beef stew and noodles, salmon salad and a cherry tart. Edith Schleiff sat next to us and exclaimed that she was thrilled with the trip and was happy she made the decision to join us.

November 9th—Jerusalem

We soon arrived at Tel Aviv and everyone was excited, but it was 10 PM and we were all pretty weary and not looking forward to the two hour trip to Jerusalem. During the trip which was on the Freedom Road, we were able to see the old trucks that were still kept on the side of the road to remind all the young people about the war of 1948.

Finally arrived at the King David Hotel at midnight and sadly I learned that our luggage would not be forthcoming until around 3 AM, so I had to sleep in a slip and bra, only to be awakened when the luggage finally arrived. This was rather a nuisance since we had to be up at 8 AM to be on time for our bus trip.

November 10th—Friday—Jerusalem

By golly we managed to be on time even though breakfast consisted of a taste of a roll and a sip of tea. Before we left for the bus I called the hotel operator to inquire about the temperature. She said it would be around 70 degrees. I then asked what it was now and she said "less", which was a typical Israeli response.

We finally boarded the bus enroute to see some of the wonders of the Israeli world. Our guide told us that to be in Jerusalem on a Friday was a blessing. He then quoted a well known expression. "Jerusalem is the city of god, the temple is the house of god, and the shabbos is the gift of god". He also said that "people don't keep the sabboth, the sabboth keeps the people".

The whole group rode directly to the spot where the Mandelbaum gate used to be. However it had been torn down since the 6 day war. Barbed wire was still present in certain areas, and there were also fox holes. I actually entered a fox hole and found an Arab boot left behind during the 6 day war and also a dented Arab vegetable can which I brought home to New York.

The entire area through which we rode appeared to be pale beige, very spacious, very hilly and very rubbley and it was all part of the Judean Hills.

We then passed the hotel Intercontinental which had been built by the Arabs and is now in Israel. Many little Arab children gathered around us begging for money and trying to sell us beads in a most persuasive manner and it was quite difficult to refuse them.

Next we visited Mt. Scopus where the original Hebrew University stood and so did the old Hadassah Hospital. Now just the ruins remain although they are expected to rebuild the hospital in the near future.

The Intercontinental by the way was built on a desecrated Jewish cemetery, and the slope below was still littered with open graves and knocked down tombstones. A most depressing sight to behold.

We also passed the MT. of Olives, where just beyond were ashes from some of Hitler's victims which were found in concentration camp graves, and were interred here to lie in peace! This was certainly most depressing to witness.

Then in the Valley below we were shown "the Dome of the Rock", a golden ball of ancient Christian fame, and also the "Gethsemane Garden" and Church of Absalom" where Jesus was arrested and taken away to be crucified.

The great moment of seeing "The wailing Wall" or "Western Wall" as it is now called, finally arrived. It was indeed a thrill to see it, especially since they have recently excavated a greater portion of it in one section, since the 6 day war. They expect to keep digging an additional 50 feet in hopes of finding the remains of the first temple of Solomon. The existing wall is the remains of the second temple.

The custom at the wall was to pray and push a little paper with a personal prayer written on it, in a tiny crevice, which we all did. There were many people lamenting audibly in Hebrew, seemingly in tremendous grief and apparent bereavement standing at the wall, and there were also people simply uttering general prayers. All in all it was a most moving experience.

We were then warned to stick close to our guide as we proceeded through the old Arab market place. This was an unbelievable sight of crowded, ancient world stalls, one on top of the other in a narrow path of cobblestones, donkeys being led by 6 year old kids, old blind men with sticks for canes, turbaned Arabs smoking pot or hashish, filthy children, and people in dirty ugly doorways selling their wares, consisting of ugly food of unknown origin, sides of beef with entrails hanging down, pottery, vegetables, toys, fabric, hardware, and absolutely every conceivable other items.

We also saw huge heads of cabbage as big as basket balls or even bigger and radishes as big as apples. (The farming ability of these people is truly amazing).

However it was a fearsome experience walking through this area, and one which I would not care to do alone. This continued easily for a few blocks until we emerged at the site of Jesus's grave and it was truly hard to believe what we were seeing. Then we entered the church which was built by Queen Helena, the wife of King Constantine. She came here and discovered the cross upon which Jesus was crucified (supposedly) and also the ones of the two thieves who were crucified with him and she presumably buried them separately.

We also saw the place in the entrance of the church where Jesus was washed after he was cut down, and the place upstairs where he was crucified, in which there is now an altar, a cross with a portrait of him, and a small amount of the remains of the cross marking the exact spot where it took place.

Ultimately we walked down into the "cave" where the holy sepulcher was located and entered a small low ceilinged chamber (we had to bend low to enter) wherein lies Jesus's marble grave in a raised position. It really seems beyond belief to imagine that this was actually the remains of Christ and

I couldn't help whispering to myself "are you really there Jesus".

These various places are called "stations" and were the places where Jesus stopped to rest on the way to the crucification. There were 14 in all. After we emerged we found ourselves back at the end of the Arab marketplace where Al bought a small goatskin rug for $5.00. I think Nancy will like it under her coffee table. Then we wearily returned to the Hotel for lunch. Chicken soup and rice, veal chops, carrot salad, and fruit. All was very dull and tasteless! (Israelis need to find better cooks)

At last we went back to the bus amidst a sudden downpour and rode to the J.C.C.Y. building which Reggie Port told me to investigate. This was a beautiful new place filled with many pictures drawn by children, and where we heard an interesting lecture by a man who was hired to take us on a temple tour. He was dramatic and enlightening about the different sects of Judaism and the various forms of worship.

He explained how the Yemenites were the caravan tribe and prayed as they rode the camels, and since they entered the city on foot when they arrived, they had to learn their prayers by heart, as they had no books, so each person learned a portion. In this way the different prayers were handed down to many generations. They still know their prayers by heart and pray in this manner.

The Sephardics were a more emotional people and prayed in a dramatic way with many gestures and much expression. Their temple was disguised as a Moslem church in order to deceive the Moslems who would not permit them to pray in Hebrew. Therefore they had a double arc with the Holy Torah on one side and the Koran on the other. They also had an extra little window above the regular ones for a lookout to observe if the Moslems were coming, as the Jews were probably praying forbidden prayers. Green was the Moslem holy color so they had to have their Torah covered in green. Again this was to deceive the Moslems.

In the Bucharan temple there were colorful curtains over the arc. Hot pink or red was used to ward off evil and green and blue were lucky colors. Also Persian rugs covered all the seats and floors, and afforded a very gay appearance to the little room, which was actually the size of most of their temples. There were 465 temples in Jerusalem, each representing different tribes of Israel and the Beamas were generally in the middle.

The Hassidic Jews said their prayers hidden in songs so as to deceive their enemies and no matter what the melody was they would be saying the same prayer. We also saw the Hassidic Mikvah with all the Jews coming out with their wet towels and covering their faces so they would not be photographed.

We were almost caught in the area after sundown and had to have the bus speed up in order to get out of the region before we were being stoned.

Actually we made it with two minutes to spare. We were also told that every temple all over the world is built facing west as that is the direction of the Western Wall in Jerusalem, there is however one exception which is the last one we visited and it is situated with Mt. Scopus one side and the Mt of Olives on the other. This temple sect felt that god is everywhere and it didn't matter about direction.

The Mt. Of Olives indicates peace and perpetual life, as the olive tree never dies, and Mt. Scopus is representative of the military and bloodshed. After learning so much we returned to the King David Hotel and gratefully snoozed for a while.

After we awakened we went down to the cocktail party which was held in our honor and then had dinner with the Gould's, Keat's, Landis's and ourselves. This dinner was really mediocre—noodle soup, gefilte fish, turkey, (canned) carrots, red cabbage and compote. We then sat around and chatted a bit and finally went to bed for much needed sleep. I must say the Israeli cuisine leaves a great deal to be desired, Paris it is not!

Oh yes, we also saw the Hassidic Jews wearing fur hats which apparently represent the 12 tribes of Israel with 12 markings inside and lined in blue to indicate the sky. Everything seems to have a meaning here.

Saturday, November 11th—Jerusalem

We awakened quite refreshed at 10 A.M. and ordered breakfast upstairs. We just had prunes and tea. That was it! (We certainly won't gain weight in Israel).

Then we went to the art museum. This was a really wonderful place with many, many interesting treasures. We also took pictures of Ada Zakin's relatives' names over the entrance doorway (Wix) and were almost in trouble as no cameras are allowed. We saw a really fine art collection including Picasso's, Cezanne's, Van Gogh's, Gorky, Kokoshka, Matisse, Degas etc. Also we were in the Billy Rose Garden and saw the original Venetian temple which was removed intact. It was a truly beautiful little place. They had old circumcision tools and cups and ceremonial effects, plus pre-historical tools and ceramics. There were old rugs in a wealth of colors plus old ceremonial clothing lavishly embroidered and some finely woven lace. Everything was laid out in a most attractive fashion and we understood that in the 6 day war the entire place was cleaned out and everything was buried in the basement, all within 2 hours.

It was so exciting to see the many familiar names over the various donated items, which came from all over the world and many of which we recognized.

Finally we went back to the hotel for lunch with the Verby's, where we had salad, cheese cake and tea, it was poor quality as is all the food here. We sat around for most of the afternoon as it rained a good deal of the time, but then around 5PM we went to a little art gallery down the street to hear Mr. Freiman, the Israeli Jackie Mason. He was absolutely a wonderful raconteur, and he told stories at an incredible rate of speed with typical poignant gestures of the average Israeli Jew and we were told he makes a recording which we will try to buy. He also told a story of how people in Israel usually ask tourists "do you come from America or New York"? and then explained the difference between rich people and richer people. One is ungushtupt, the second is aufmergesucht.

Again we returned to the Hotel for dinner. It was quite mediocre as usual and I have already forgotten the menu—Thank Heavens! (Israel is a diet country out of necessity!)

We then started to go to the YMCA across the street to hear a concert, but decided to go to the JCCY for folk dancing instead. We stayed there a very short time as it was not an exhibition, it was just for tourist instruction, however we met two young girls there who took us on a public bus to Hillel House to watch the young people dance. That was really great fun, although it smelled like a gymnasium. One of the girls was a Brandeis student on a six month program, Susan Levine from Steubenville, Ohio. Then we went back to the Hotel for tea and raisin cake with the Verbys, Keats and Weinribs.

Sunday, November 12th

This was a wonderful day! We saw so much it was hard to believe. We started out in the morning to see the Judean Hills and the Dead Sea Scrolls and it was extremely fascinating to see them. They were found in caves in urns and in goatskin water vessels, and in leather pouches with their colors intact, and also in cloth fabrics, red, yellow and green. They were two thousand years old and really amazing! There was the first marriage contract, the first real estate contract and laws of disciple governing behavior in cooperative living. Truly a beautiful memorial.

Our next stop was the Kennedy Memorial which was lovely, high on a hill like a birthday cake with 50 windows representing all the states and with the eternal flame in the middle. The Kennedy family had not yet been to see it however, although Schmoyl the bus driver drove Bob Kennedy six years ago, who liked Schmoyl and sent for him to come to New York. All his expenses were paid for a month's trip so he went to Chicago, Florida, Canada and Paris before returning home.

The next visit was to Yad Vashem which was the memorial of the 6 million dead from Auschwitz, etc. This was very very sad. It had large stones all around a circular building and almost looked like people's heads clumped together.

After that we went on to the Hadassah Medical Center which is a wonderful hospital facility. We were taken on a tour by a charming girl and saw many familiar names on the doors of the hospital rooms, mostly names of people from New York. A great many from Long Island and Woodmere, etc. The hospital is extremely modern with four floors below ground for protection. Also there was a chapel with beautiful Chagall windows, four of which were damaged in the 6 day war.

We then wearily proceeded to the Knesset (Parliament), a magnificent building beautifully spacious with bronze doors crafted by an Italian artist (Palumbo). There were interesting lighting effects in the Board room which included lights over each chair and it was a rectangular apparatus. We also saw the Chagall mosaics on the walls of the reception hall and on the floor as well.

There was a design for a tapestry depicting the flight from Jerusalem etc. and in addition there was a most interesting building concept for apartment houses that we noticed en route. A 7 story house built on a hill which had the entrance on the 4th floor so people only had to walk two flights was very interesting and there was another entrance on the bottom of the hill for the first three floors.

The remarkable thing about Jerusalem was the way it was terraced dating from Roman times in order to farm little strips of land and to prevent erosion. The whole bowl or valley is that way, which was most fascinating to see.

We finally left the town and went back to the hotel to the Grill Room for lunch and it was quite good for a change. There we had hors d'oeuvres. Artichoke, mushroom and asparagus, then gazpacho soup, sliced beef and fruit compote.

Big excitement! While we were eating Moishe Dayan walked in and we could hardly believe it. He was extremely good looking and charming. Al asked him for his autograph and he kindly wrote his name on a piece of paper. Then everyone nearby came to gape at him. We tried to take his picture but he was reticent, nevertheless Debbie

Morganstern borrowed my camera and he posed for her. But unfortunately the flash did not work. Too bad, but at least we had his signature.

We then went upstairs to wait for Samuel Schweky—Moishe's brother. He arrived and was gracious and pleasant. In fact he took us on a three hour tour of the old city and this was absolutely fabulous. We went through narrow winding streets in the market place, through alleys where dirty children played with makeshift toys in absolute filth and squalor. Some of the children (Arab) were beautiful even through the dirt on their faces.

Then we saw the parts of the old city that used to be for the Jews before 1948 and even where Samuel was born. His family were Sabras from hundreds of years back, which was fascinating to learn.

We also entered the "Dome of the Rock" which was an Arab mosque. It was built around the rock upon which Abraham was about to sacrifice his son Isaac, and then we actually saw the rock itself in the center of which was a natural hole where Isaac's blood was supposed to drip through. We had to enter the mosque without shoes and stepped on rugs that King Hussein gave to the Dome last year. The Dome is made of aluminum painted gold with real gold on top.

We also went to the old mosque where King Solomon's courtyard was and where King Hussein always came to pray in a separate little place. Ten thousand Arabs come there to pray every Friday and face the east but the women pray in another separate room. There were huge marble columns in the mosque plus a beautifully decorated ceiling.

We then saw where Virgin Mary was born which was right inside the gate where the Israeli army broke through into the Arab compound during the 6 day war. Also one hundred Israeli soldiers were killed right there and several jeeps with soldiers inside went through the streets while we were there so we were really living through history in the making

Believe it or not we bought another fur goatskin rug in a butcher shop! Samuel speaks just like an Arab therefore the people in the area believe that he is one, so he was able to take us to a new Arab section where we had coffee (Turkish and awful) and tea. There were also many tourist travel agencies in the area as well as several banks. It was a scary and strange feeling to be there and it was so different from Jerusalem in the Jewish section.

We then went to see Jane's mother-in-law. Her family lived quite simply but were nice people, very hospitable and pleasant. We had lunch with them which included lentil soup, veal chop, spaghetti, boiled zucchini, boiled carrots and boiled beets.

We left there about 6:30 PM and were able to pass through the Hassidic section where we bought mezuzahs and a tallis for Al's brother Harry, then we finally returned to the Hotel thoroughly exhausted but thrilled with everything we had experienced.

We also heard that Sid Lippman and Sol Berger were in Jericho and had become involved in a border incident. It seems they took two wounded soldiers to the hospital, but we never found out what actually happened.

Then for the first time Al and I had dinner alone but had some dessert with the Verby's as it was Stanley's 50th birthday and so to bed and to write this little tale of the day's activities. I'm really beat!

Monday—November 13th En Route to Tel Aviv

We left Jerusalem in a flurry of activity but the Keats's stayed behind as they were ill with "tourista", as were most everyone else during the trip.

En route we passed Rachel's tomb but could not visit it as it did not open until 9:30 AM, and there was a big line waiting outside anyway. Then we continued on to Bethlehem where we went to the Church of Nativity and saw the actual place down in a cave like area where Jesus was born. This was a very old church, dark and dreary with many pure gold pictures in the forefront.

We were off again to visit the town of Mt. Hebron, a fascinating place where no Jew had been in Abraham's tomb for over 2000 years and which was an unusual place, like a series of courtyards in white, red and black marble. Rebecca's tomb was inside a large area, and Abraham, Leah and Jacob were in an outside portion, which resembled cages behind bars in exposed type crypts.

Then we passed through the countryside, which was mostly caves and there were Arab pup tents, and stones in terraces as far as the eye could see. We also saw the place where Shlomey (the driver of our bus) fought. The land there was full of mud huts with rural farmers working on the ground using crude hand plows and donkeys, (these people really had difficult lives).

We also passed Israeli soldiers eating grapes and drinking whisky and they were all very strong looking boys. Then at last we saw the Negev Desert where there were tamarant trees and eucalyptus planted by the J.NF. at the beginning of the desert. There were also many Bedouins (nomads) who liked to live in tents and not in houses, even though barracks had been built for them. They put their animals in the barracks and they slept in tents alongside, which was unusual and strange indeed.

The earth in this area was dry and parched in tones of beige, tawny and camel and the vegetation was poorly planted. There were also many caves and wadis and the earth was so old looking and dreary. It was a most dismal place indeed.

We then found out that not only the Israelis can serve in the army but also the Druses (half Arabs). However they hate the Arabs and consider it to be a blessing if they kill them.

During our ride Rafe, our guide suddenly hopped out of the bus to pick a pineapple appearing plant "Agava" out of which tequila and rape is made. He also told us that this plant is so strong it cannot be torn apart, which was only one of the amazing things we were learning on this trip.

Next stop was "Arad", a town of prefabrication houses. It was quite industrial and was built by the U.J.A and the government will give anyone free real estate if he or she builds a house there within a year. While we were there we had a good lunch at the Hotel Arad. It was Bourrekas (pastry filled with meat) then beef with rice, carrots and fruit. The town was a most modern city and is in the heart of the Negev Desert.

Great News! We were finally at the "Dead Sea" which had blue, blue water, no motion whatsoever and anyone who swam there floated on top of the water. The Dead Sea is in the deepest part of the world. It has the highest amount of evaporation and much salt and potash and our hands felt dry and clammy just by being exposed to the air.

Next we arrived at Beersheba which means "the promise of the wall". There is an existing story that when Abraham wanted to prevent people from stealing his water he asked for help from the king and because it was granted to him, he gave the king seven sheep.

We also found out that there were just about three thousand people living there in 1917 and since 1956 there are approximately 85,000. The houses were built on stilts with a play area below for the children. Also there is now a huge hospital and cinema theatre, plus the largest synagogue in Israel.

We then stopped for coffee at the Desert Inn Hotel which was a nice resort and then continued on to the Dan Hotel in Tel Aviv. After arriving there at 6:30 PM we bathed and then dressed to meet Jerry Becker's cousins and we had a little snack with them at the California Bar, a cute little place on Dizengoff Street (the main street in Tel Aviv). They were making a movie in the area and therefore many people were gathered just to watch, so we just ate some cannelloni.

Then we visited a friend of Mr. Bizer (Al's jewelry friend from New York). She was a lady oculist—Dr. Hershberg, and she had a beautiful apartment which contained many wonderful paintings and old rugs and also she was a most charming person. By that time however we were extremely tired as we had walked all over trying to find her apartment. Everybody in Israel walks and walks and walks!

November 14th, Tuesday—Tel Aviv

This morning we were still tired even after a night's sleep and just managed to catch the bus after finally having a nice breakfast. (Delicious melon and rolls.)

However we then saw the main portion of the city, The Habinah, National Theatre, Main Auditorium, and Helena Rubenstein's Art Pavilion (called the Lipstick Building). They were all situated together in the square.

We also saw the fort and then the gorgeous blue Mediterranean. After that came Ancient Jaffa, which had narrow streets and a crowded market place where they sold old horrible clothes and vegetables. The artist colony there however, was charming with many "sign of the zodiac" ceramic street signs

Once again we went back to the hotel for a while and soon went out for a stroll with Marcia and Milton Landis, and then wandered through many interesting streets and had a piecemeal lunch. It was corn on the cob right out of a hot pot on the street, marvelous roasted almonds, soup and rolls in one café and finally cake and tea in another place, then after nibbling around town I finally went to a beauty parlor (Becky's Salon) for a much needed shampoo. I also bought a wild watercolor with a Picasso like face and then returned to the hotel for a rest period. It was a weary day to say the least.

Nevertheless we still had the stamina to go to a gallery in the hotel which we visited while waiting for Sophie Rothstein's cousin, Isabel. She was charming and lovely in appearance and we had dinner with her in the Grill Room of the Hotel Dan.

Our dinner there consisted of mushrooms prepared in an onion, garlic, lemon vinegar sauce, followed by broiled lamb chops, delicious baked tomato and cauliflower accompanied by onions, pimentos and peppers chopped fine and there was a great melon for dessert, somewhat like the French melon, small and sweet.

All of us then walked to Dizengoff Street and afterwards we went to Jaffa to the art colony. There were really charming places to see, galleries, ceramic shops and very interesting handcrafts. Everything was beautiful so it was most difficult to make a purchase. However I finally bought a small brass brazier for candy. It will be useful and was attractive besides. I also saw some beautiful paintings but they were extremely expensive, and besides the place was so busy we could not get the attention of a salesperson long enough to consider making a purchase. I guess I'll have to go back again tomorrow. I am now slightly nauseous so I had some tea and went to bed.

November 15th, Wednesday—Tel Aviv

At last we had a leisurely day with no commitments except that we bought an op art painting this A.M. in the hotel gallery and then visited Sophie's cousin again. She really was friendly and sweet, just like Sophie.

I walked on Dizengoff this afternoon by myself as Al went off to buy kiddish cups (although he was unable to find any) and I felt a little daring while strolling along alone.

Then we had lunch at the hotel with Edith Schleiff and the Landis's. We also sat in the sun for a while and had dinner with Sol Bergman, etc. Afterwards we returned to Jaffa where the Landis's made several purchases but we were unable to find anything of interest. So we really spent a most quiet and much needed restful day. However we are leaving here tomorrow and it will mean an entire day on the bus. (Exhaustion here we come!)

November 16th, Thursday En Route to Haifa

We left Tel Aviv after breakfast and since this was a lovely sunny day we drove to Natanya, a suburban summer resort named for Nathan Strauss who started Macy's Department Store. We stopped there for "coffee in and coffee out" and while there I bought a lovely copper teapot and then returned to the bus, and we continued to drive through a fairly cultivated countryside with banana groves and orange trees for a considerable distance. The bananas were covered with plastic bags to prevent the birds from eating them.

Incidentally in Natanya we noticed that the homes were heated with a solar system. There was a screen like device attached to water tanks on the roofs, which heats the water in the thermos tanks and holds the heat in the water for days. It was a most innovative system which would be great in America.

On to Caesaria to view the ruins left by the Romans and Byzantines. We saw the most interesting "tel" just barely excavated as the entire area was still being worked on. We also saw the auditorium partly reconstructed which is facing the Mediterranean, and it had perfect acoustics. One of our bus passengers sang a song to prove it.

Then we glimpsed the ancient moat and the aqueduct in the central part of the city with two huge statues flanking the main street. They had their heads removed, as was the custom when the Turks took over any Roman area.

We also found some small pieces of pottery chips with grooves in them, and a piece of marble, which came from the ground or a pillar no doubt.

One interesting thing took place next. We went to the golf course which was quite lovely and Al teed off while I took a picture of him hitting the ball. (A great shot!)

We then had lunch at the Ramada Hotel and had delicious barley soup, not so good beef, peas and potatoes, but we ate the fruit we bought in Natanya. An "Amana" or "Sabra" fruit. It was delicious especially with lemon juice. Then we sat in the sun for a while and afterwards went back to the bus en route to see the Rothchild Memorial and tomb. This was in a magnificent park with iron gates decorated with grapes (indicating wine products). The entire area is somewhat like the Metropolitan Museum dining pavilion (marble with pool sections) and then the tomb itself has one large glass window shaped like a heart.

Next we stopped at Ein Hod to see the art works but there were so many people it was impossible to see anything, besides it was really much too hectic. I was beginning to think "enough is enough"!

We finally reached Mt. Carmel and began a most exciting and nerve racking drive through hair raising curves on twisted narrow roads. There was a majestic view of the mountains with the sight of many caves of pre-historic origin. I was told that men and women used to live in these caves and were sheltered therein. I really can't imagine how crude their lives used to be.

As we drove along we passed valleys and high mountains that were indescribable and the sunset was a glorious vision to behold. I never knew Israel was so lovely and this trip was really an eye opener.

Eventually we arrived at the Dan Carmel hotel, weary but exuberant. It was a beautiful hotel and we were able to obtain a nice room with a fabulous view of the harbor which was magnificent to see especially at night.

We had to go to sleep for a while as we were quite tired from the bus trip, and finally had dinner at Bilyor, a nice restaurant but quite crowded. We had good melon but the chicken was not so good so we went back to the hotel for tea and a bit of conversation. I also found 65 cents in my chair (American money). We are extremely tired now so goodnight.

Friday, November 17th Haifa

Awakened early and dashed downstairs to get the front seats on the bus as we had been sitting in the back all week. The redhead who always sat up front was a little put out because she felt entitled, however she took the second seat near Schloyme (I think she had a crush).

We then visited Nazareth and saw the church of Annunciation where Mary conceived Jesus and where Joseph had his workshop. It was the most incredible sight. We also wandered through the Arab Bazaar and bought a little brass camel and candleholder, which I know I will treasure at home.

One person in our group got on a donkey while wearing an Arab hat and then we all took pictures of him. Al bought an Arab hat too and it was a lot of fun.

Then we went on to Cana where Deborah fought the Battle of Jethro. The next stop was Lake Tiberious on the Sea of

Galilee. This was a perfect little jewel of a place. It had sparkling water of a brilliant blue, and was small and lovely. It was supposedly where Jesus was thought to have walked on the water. Although according to Rafie our guide, that was just an optical illusion.

We also saw the church where Jesus supposedly multiplied the loaves and fish. The original mosaics are still on the ground and we took pictures of it.

Our next stop was the synagogue of the 1st century A.D., which is the second oldest synagogue in the world, and had the original pillars in a Greek key design (Nazi) and also had fruit, star and rosette designs. The original mill grinder and olive oil press were also still there and in great condition.

We then had a pretty good lunch at kibbutz Nof Ginosar where the food was wholesome and really not bad (for a change) and the Kebutz itself was a truly nice place which was mostly filled with women and young children.

So at last after a busy day we returned to the hotel where we arranged to put on a little skit this coming Sunday and we became very busy writing songs.

Then we had cocktails with Marcia and Milton. (It was her birthday) and we had our dinner after which we met Al's cousin Gedalia Gonan, a charming person who took us to his son's home (Chava and Zvi Gonan). They were a really fine couple who were entertaining 20 local people, including a judge (district court), a French ophthalmologist with a darling wife Andreé Micheyn, a lawyer, an engineer and a wealthy builder from South Africa. They were all most interesting and intellectual people. The Gonans were hospitable indeed and we felt like we were in Lawrence. It was also nice to be with relatives.

The lawyer knew Julian Venezky very well which was a surprise. Then Chava served a hot boiled potato filled with chopped lamb with rosemary and pignola nuts, then another hot hors d'oeuvre and finally tea and cake, which included brownies, chocolate cake and fruit cake and were all home made. It was a wonderful evening and we came back to the hotel quite late. Oh dear we were tired and realized we had to rise early tomorrow—very little sleep again.

November 18th, Saturday—Haifa

Made a date to have dinner at Gedalia Gonan's home which was beautiful. They had lovely furnishings and beautiful rugs and apparently he had a thriving business, an automobile dealership. They were most hospitable to us and after an extremely nice dinner his wife gave me an envelope to take home, with the same mushroom soup which she had served us and which was delicious. Naturally it was dry so I could take it back to New York. In her kitchen she had a plant that went from the bottom of one window all the way around to the top and across and down again to the bottom of the second window. It was an unusual arrangement to say the least and it was great to have been with them.

November 19th, Sunday

We were finally en route back to New York and we all sang the songs we wrote on the plane trip home. They were as follows:

A motley medley en route to Kennedy Airport to the tune of the (Volga Boatman)

Oi that long Schlep, oi that long Schlep
Seemed like 40 days and nights
Where were the non stop flights?

(Gilbert & Sullivan)

3 little maids from school

3 little seats in a row had we
The one near the window had to pee
The one on the aisle said "find a tree"
"Or else for god's sake"—no more tea
Our little group was all so weary
Some so tired—almost teary
Who'd a thunk it could be so dreary
Waiting in Cologne

Athens (Matchmaker)

Worry beads, worry beads help us get rid
Of our mate's mishagoses, their egos and id

Worry beads, worry beads, help us to find
The comforts we left behind

Jerusalem (California here I come)

Jerusalem, here we come,
This is where we started from
Your temples, your churches and wailing wall
The people, the spirit, we love them all
Because you've had your share of war and strife
We wish you now a better life
Jerusalem—we love you

Tel Aviv—(Mandelay tune)

On the road to Tel Aviv
Where the jewelry merchants thieve
Where the pins and rings sell just like honey
In every little dive
Here the girls all spent much money
And the traveler checks grew thin
And the men who smiled so broadly
Now each wear a sickly grin

All Over Israel (Little Brown Jug)

Little Brown Pill
How I need you
The perfect cure for the wandering Jew
Always running—miss or hit
Because we have no time to s-t

Galilee (By The Sea)

Galilee, Galilee by the beautiful sea
With your flies and your heat
You're not really for me
We all wanted to leave the bus
It's not for us
All we want is the W.C.
And so it's lunch for 2 or 6 or 8
We Jews all love to congregate
We eat—then run to the gift shop quick
God forbid we miss a trick

Haifa (Di Di Einu)

Hi Hi Haifa, Hi Hi Haifa, Hi Hi Haifa
So high up in the hills
As we ride along the highway
Everyone is yelling Oy Vey
Past the caves and gorgeous skyway
I wouldn't drive if I had my way
Up to Mt. Carmel
Hi Hi Haifa, Hi Hi Haifa, Hi Hi Haifa
So high up in the hills

Safed

We have suffered, we have suffered
We have suffered in Safed today
We will never get together
As to who is gonna go or stay

Prayer for Sabena

Oh give me a trip where there's room for my grip
Let me fly straight from here to New York
Then I'll never complain bout the Long Island train
Where the brotherhood members all squawk
Oh home I want to go home
Even though it means "back to work"
I'll be nice to my wife
And I'll live the good life
Just like every Five townie jerk

Finally we arrived in New York weary, tired and thoroughly exhausted, but filled with exuberant tales to convey to our friends and families about the wonders we experienced and had seen on this marvelous trip. Nothing can ever compare to the never to be forgotten thrills that Greece and especially Israel provided us. They will last for our entire lifetimes. Shalom!

LAKE COMO—VILLA D'ESTE
Monday, October 7, 1968

Once again we were off to Europe but a little apprehensive as my old superstition regarding #7 kept popping into my head. However I had to take the bull by the horns sooner or later so we were taking the trip anyway!

We had a pleasant flight although Al and I didn't get much sleep. Lucky us though, the 3rd seat in our row was not occupied so we had ample space.

Unfortunately we arrived in Milan amidst a heavy fog which never quite lifted and soon it (as my ears detected) dissolved into a heavy rainfall.

We arrived at the hotel at 10:30 AM after an unexciting auto ride (we were picked up at the airport by the hotel car). Oh yes—we met the Portnoff Boy on the flight (he was on his honeymoon). Also on the flight was Audrey Schulman from Gina Paoli with her designer. He was a gorgeous gay guy dressed completely in Cardin. He was very chic, wearing many rings, an Edwardian jacket, nail headed shoes and a Donegal tweed suit, really trés, trés façionable.

Tuesday, October 8th—Como

The hotel was gorgeous to behold. It had old world splendor and gentility and weary though we were, we had a cup of tea and then tried to change our rooms. But finally after inspecting several others we decided to remain in the original one.

Sasha Ritter sent us magnificent flowers, most unusual zinnias, completely unlike ours in America. They were thickly petaled, healthy, strong and full bodied in a rich color. They seemed to be an unknown variety and were truly beautiful and of course we were pleased by her thoughtfulness

Then we both took sleeping pills and slept for five hours, and after dressing for dinner we went to the bar which was extremely pleasant, and it had a most talented girl singer.

For dinner we had lobster bisque, wonderful grilled tiny veal chops, and potatoes as thin as tooth picks, and grilled tomatoes. The dessert was baked pears in wine. Everything was most delicious and enjoyable after which we then called Kenny in Florence and all was well with him, thank heavens.

We then stayed in the entertainment room for an hour or so and listened to that same cute girl singer and after a while we happily went to bed. Unfortunately it immediately started teeming but I certainly hoped it would clear the next day. However as our taxi driver said "Sol" is coming, and I presumed he would be right.

Wednesday—October 9th Lake Como

Thank heavens it became a lovely day—cool but the sun was shining. We had breakfast downstairs and then went to the golf course for a short time so Al could hit some balls.

Then we took a boat trip to La Comencia for lunch. This was a picturesque little place on the only island on the lake, where we ate on a terrace and was served the same lunch as everyone else. There were no individual choices and the host was a jovial plump man who was wearing an amusing stocking cap.

For lunch we had a sliced half of a tomato, antipasto, grilled trout, fried chicken, ice cream with pears in wine and after we finished eating, the host rang a cow bell indicating that it was time for coffee. He then prepared some coffee for all of us on the terrace, including serving brandy as well. He also related a funny Italian folk tale after which we went to Bellagio a quaint little town with cobbled little alleys and streets, reminiscent of the Via Dolorosa in Israel, as it was completely lined with cheap little shops.

We stayed there for about an hour and then returned to Villa D'Este and enjoyed the beautiful view of the lake on the way back. I must say it was an extremely pleasant day.

Tea time was next plus a little nap that was welcome before dinner. The hotel was bustling with activity when we finally went downstairs, because a Shriner's convention had arrived en masse.

Nevertheless we were able to have a lovely dinner. There was stracciatelli soup, grilled steak with finely sliced mushrooms, which was served with tomatoes and eggplant, minced herbs and spices (oregano and bread crumbs) and little potatoes. They also had delicious quiche Lorraine, and finally fresh fruit (we certainly spend a lot of time eating).

We then went to the lounge and enjoyed the evening with a nice couple from Ossining, New York whom we met last night. They were extremely good dancers and well traveled and they told us they intend going home on the final sailing of the Queen Elizabeth. He was an Actuary and both of them were most attractive and charming.

The band was really great and played a terrific selection of songs with lots of rhythm. Ho Hum! Time to go to bed as tomorrow will be a hectic day as we expect to leave here at 8:30 AM for our trip to Valenza Po to see Mr. Iberti and the jewelry houses.

Thursday, October 10th—Como

We awakened just in time to have breakfast at 8:00 AM and then left for Valenza. It was a little more brisk today but delightful at Villa D'Este. The sun was shining and in general we thought it would wind up being a lovely day. However a half hour onto the highway everything changed. A heavy fog descended almost like a cloud of smoke. It was really frightening as our driver was not sure he could continue and the more we drove the worse it got. We could not see a thing on either side of the road and it turned out to be an awful day for driving.

Finally though we passed the Po River and like magic, the sun came out, the fog lifted and at last we reached Valenza.

We went to the jewelry exhibition hall first to see the various manufacturer's displays, and then called Mr.Iberti who met us at the Esmeralda hotel for lunch. We had the best risotto with mushrooms and parmesan cheese. It was thick, almost like gruel, then had veal mornay with spinach and mixed vegetables, zucchini, onions, tomatoes, peppers and eggplant. Finally we were served a candied baked pear. Everything was wonderful.

Then we started visiting different jewelers. We walked all over the whole town for two hours and after ordering several things including a lion enamel bracelet for myself, we had a gelati, and finally got back on the road home. This time we took the auto strada which was much better, and thank heavens there was no more fog.

We arrived back at the hotel at 6:45 PM just in time to have a welcoming hot shower and a little nap.

Again we had a great dinner. This time it was barley soup, sliced sturgeon with potato salad accompanied by tiny peas and string beans. Then there was sliced roast beef, stuffed artichokes, potatoes and ice cream in a meringue sandwich with chocolate on top,. It was all very good and was guaranteed to make a person gain weight!

We also spoke to Kenny again and made arrangements to meet him in Rome on Saturday. Then I wrote some postcards and went to bed.

Friday October 11th—Como, Lugano and Milan

We had breakfast at Ville D'esté and it was another beautiful day. It's too bad that we had to leave as it was really delightful here. But we had to move on.

Again we had the same car and driver (Joseph) and he drove us to Lugano. It was fun to cross the border into Swizzeria. The roads were clean and picturesque with mountains all around. We then drove into Campione which was a Little Italian village in the middle of Switzerland. Casinos were the big business in the town, and the people were completely Italian within the Swiss surroundings.

We finally arrived in Lugano just in time for lunch. This place was a lovely resort on the lake with lots of hotels and outdoor cafes and it seemed to be a bustling little town. Our lunch at Bianchi was quite good and included eggplant Sicilian and raspberries with ice cream. Once again we returned to Como and bought some ties and some pretty scarves. Como is the silk center of Italy and supposedly everything is of good quality and beautiful as well.

We were on the road again! This time to Milan. Our room at the Palace Hotel was a great disappointment. There was no shower and the room was small but thank heavens we then went to Gianinos for dinner and it was marvelous! I had a mixture of green and white noodles with mushrooms and cheese and then grilled scampi with tartar sauce. Dessert was St Honoré cake. I fully expected to gain five pounds on this trip. The restaurant was quite large with glassed in open kitchens, huge copper hoods over the ovens with many burners in the middle of the room, just like a school kitchen. The many waiters were diligently scrubbing the counters when we left the restaurant which was certainly not like New York restaurants. It was a really lovely evening and then we met a nice man from Connecticut with whom we shared a cab. He makes nuts and bolts and hopes to merge his firm with one in Milan.

We did a little shopping on Via Manzoni when we got to Milan. It was a beautiful avenue of shops and they had everything of a fine quality and it was all nicely displayed. We also walked to the Principe E Savoia Hotel which was just a shade nicer than the Palace but then we had to go to sleep as the plane was leaving at 10:30 AM Domani.

Saturday—October 12th—Milan

We awakened to a fog that was so all encompassing that I could not see five feet away and of course we presumed that our flight would not be able to take off, so we had breakfast on the roof restaurant and hopefully tried to think "clear".

However, we decided to go to the airport anyway and then had to be transferred to Malpensa, (the other airport was called Linarte). Finally at noon we took off and arrived in Rome at

1:00PM. There the sun was shining and it was delightfully warm.

We barely caught the bus to town and then met Kenny and Janis at our hotel. Kenny was a little thin but seemed fine so that was good. We bumped into Beverly Glaubman and the Dimstons in the lobby and met Stanley Elkins and Dorothy and Milton Schulman on Via Condotti where we walked after our lunch, which we had at our hotel (spaghetti with clam sauce).

The Via Condotti was lovely and we really enjoyed walking there and perusing the many beautiful shops. Finally we went back to our hotel where Al took a nap and I went to Eva of Rome. This time I had a rather poor hairdo but at least my hair was clean.

Happily we went to Tre Scalini for dinner with Kenny and Janis and the Dimston's where we had pollo a la romano e pepperoni and once again had spaghetti with clams. There were pears for dessert. (I am starting to look like a balloon!!)

After walking around for a while we finally cabbed back to the hotel and had a much needed good night's sleep, although the lights went out a few times while we were dressing, and the shower wasn't so terrific, but the room was generally a satisfactory one.

Sunday—October 13th—Rome

Miraculously we slept late and then Kenny and Janis came for us at 11:30 AM. We went to see "Moses" again and walked through the "Forum" for a while. Then we all had lunch, at a little place off the Via Veneto, which consisted of Fettucini and pie. Again we walked (which is what we do most of the time) and finally left the kids so they could go to the station. After sitting at Doney's for a while we eventually went back to the hotel for a nap. It was a real lazy day, but we needed it.

Unexpectedly Ed and Caroline Blumberg called us and we arranged to meet them for dinner at Hosteria Del Orso with their friends the Batines (Charles and Rita) who are apparently good friends of Richard Tucker. This was quite an atmospheric place dating back to 1300. Dante lived there and many morbid tales about him emanated from the Inn (which it was originally). Our dinner was delicious. We had cannelloni (thick with cheese) steak pizziola with tiny zucchini and fresh grown skinny string beans, and then profiteroles filled with whipped cream, topped with glazed sugar and chocolate syrup for dessert. Ambrosial and fattening to say the least. It was a most pleasant evening, the weather was beautiful and all in all we had a delightful time. (All we do is enjoy ourselves!)

Monday—October 14th—Rome to Florence

We had breakfast downstairs at the hotel and then proceeded to Mr. Landsman for some golf gloves. After that I walked down to the Via Condotti and Al left me to get some information about Cannes.

We had our lunch at the hotel which consisted of bombolini (large shell shaped pasta with meat sauce and cheese), then a vegetable plate containing zucchini, eggplant sticks, carrots and spinach and finally there was Spanish melon. Everything was delicious. Oh this food!!

Next we left for the train station and got onto the train. No one was sitting next to us so it was quite relaxing. We had a lovely compartment all to ourselves and arrived in Florence at 5:30 PM We didn't see Kenny so we went directly to the hotel. Surprisingly we had an absolutely gorgeous room with 2 bathrooms in a little circle with a dressing room that had flowered chintz curtains.

Kenny arrived a few minutes after we checked in and had a shower in our bathroom. This apparently was a real treat for him.

Monday—October 14th—Florence

I then called the Perlmans and we arranged to have dinner with them and also with their friend "Yaco Di Firenze" (Kleinman). He used to live in Lawrence and now lives in Florence in order to avoid paying alimony to his wife. He took us to a wonderful native restaurant "Otellos" where we had a really marvelous salad, lasagna and then scampi and eggplant then baked pears and cake. It was an enormous dinner but really great.

I may be catching a cold but certainly hope not, although I sneezed about 35 times today.

Tuesday—October 15th—Florence

After breakfast we went to Via Turobuoni with the Perlmans and then walked around until it was time to meet Kenny at our hotel. We all had lunch at Doney's and then went to meet his "family". They were most lovely people. The lady is charming and is a very pretty "mother" and he is quite lucky to be living with them for part of his semester. We had tea and cake with them and also had a nice conversation, with Kenny as the interpreter.

His Italian is really quite good and he has a great accent as well. After walking around town a bit we stopped to buy Al some shoes and some boots for me. Both pairs were very nice. Then we went back to the hotel to rest before dinner which we had at Campodilio—Carlo no longer works there and the food was not so good, although the steak was tender. It was a quiet and uneventful evening and so to sleep.

Wednesday—October 16th—Florence

We met the Schwartzman's in the lobby this morning and had red orange juice again for breakfast—delicious! Then we meandered around for a while and also tried to buy more shoes to no avail. Finally we met Kenny for lunch at Buca Lapi. I had noodles with funghi, scampi and eggplant, all of which were delicious. We gave a coin to Carlo Ceccitelli, but I don't think it was the right fellow, the one we promised the coin to on our last trip was taller. Sadly we were not able to do too much walking after lunch as it started to rain, however we did manage to buy handbags for the girls in the office, and then relaxed for a while at the hotel.

That evening we had dinner with the Schwartzman's at the hotel. I had chicken soup, a veal chop with ham and cheese, a nice salad and fruit cup for dessert. This food is really getting to be overwhelming!

We sat in the lobby with them and also with Kenny until midnight just talking. All in all it was a most pleasant evening. Kenny brought me a gift from his "mama". It was extremely kind of her to give it to me as I admired one just like it in her home. It was a brass key holder that hangs on the kitchen wall and will be very useful and attractive as well.

Thursday—October 17th—Florence

I then went wandering with Kenny and Al this morning, and later to a jeweler just with Al. We had lunch at a little place in the Piazza Del Signora and then visited the Pitti Palace where a whole new world opened up. We saw many old favorites—Titians, Raphaels, Murillos, etc. and other beautiful items as well. This was a truly wondrous place. The ceilings almost seemed to be in relief. I met Eleanor Polinoff there and I also went to Pucci again to try making an exchange but of course they refused to do so.

I then went to the beauty parlor and the man who did my hair was pretty good, thank heavens.

That night we went to Sabatini's for dinner. As it was Janis's birthday I ordered a birthday cake but of course we had to have St. Honoré too. This was really a divine concoction with a wonderful crust, and whipped cream with shaved chocolate on top. There were éclairs with custard filling all around the cake and drizzled candy on top—mervailleuse. We also had prosciutto with figs, noodles, scampi and salad.

We met Caroline and Eddie Blumberg at the Grand Hotel later in the evening and then returned to our hotel to pack as we were leaving the next day. The lights went out again in our hotel room but the service is great and they were back on in a Jiffy.

Friday—October 18th—Florence and Nice

Kenny came to say goodbye and of course we will miss him as I am sure he will miss us. But his semester in Florence will always be a wonderful memory for him. I can't think of a greater experience for a young person.

We took the train back to Rome and after waiting two hours in the terminal we ultimately took off for Nice. Finally arrived there at 6:30 PM and were in the Hotel Negresco at 7:00 PM. The hotel was lovely in an antiquated fashion but our room left much to be desired. The bathroom was inadequate as to hooks and shelves, etc. and I also had a cold which did not lighten my spirits any, although my appetite was still good!

After settling into the room we went to "Garoc" for dinner. This was a fielding suggestion and Al's choice. As it turned out it was a bad one. It was a fish place but apparently bouillabaisse was the only good item available, and one which Al did not enjoy particularly. I had langouste which we found out later was extremely expensive and not worth it. Therefore our bill was prohibitive and only included the main dish and tea. It was certainly a far cry from "Otello" in Florence where six of us ate for the same price and the dinner there was fit for Kings.

So far the city of Nice seemed cheap and tawdry. It was like a tired empty Miami at the lower end of Collins Avenue.

However we did see an interesting art exhibit in the hotel. The artist's name was "Szigati" and he painted with his fingers a la Jackson Pollack only Lumpier. They were extremely unusual canvases and attractive as well.

We then walked around the shopping rotunda in the large room at the hotel, which seemed to be set-up in an international fashion and it was a rather clever arrangement.

Then we had tea in the coffee shop which ingeniously had many articles for sale displayed right inside the table tops under glass. Most unusual to say the least.

After that we returned to our room which proved to be quite dismal and simply went to bed. Hopefully tomorrow will prove to be a more pleasing day.

Saturday, October 19th—Nice

Claire called us in the morning and we all went to The Forum Beach. Louis the proprietor and chief cook, etc was very cute and made a fuss over us, I guess it was because he liked Claire.

We also talked with a lovely lady "Roberta" and invited her to join us for lunch. She was a widow whose husband lost most of his money in Algiers because of DeGaulle whom she violently hated. Her daughter lives in Canada and owns a ski chalet there.

We then had omelets for lunch and cinzano. By the way the beach was not a sand beach. It was comprised of little grey stones with white stripes. They were quite different in appearance and I picked up several of them that had lovely shapes which Al is going to set in gold ring settings. Nobody will ever guess what kind of "gems" they are.

In the afternoon we drove to Cannes with the Perlmans, which I liked much more than Nice. The shops there were beautiful and the hotels were gorgeous.

Our choice for dinner was a cute little restaurant near Garoc which was really good and the food was cooked around open fires. We had oysters, scampi, rice and a huge dessert in a glass. It was minced fresh fruit, sherbet, whipped cream, shaved almonds, and chocolate sauce.

We then became friendly with the French people at the next table, and finally after we laughed and talked with each other for some time, they invited us to their home tomorrow evening for an "aperitif".

They were most attractive and charming people and their names are "Madame and Monsier Armand Bousidan". He sells silks and woolens in his shop which was called "Bouchera" and it is located in Nice.

Then we drove to Beaulieu to see La Reserve which I liked. It was on the Moyenne Corniche which is a perilous road in the mountains. It was extremely winding through small areas almost like narrow lanes. However the evening was enjoyable even though I now have a cold!

Sunday, October 20th—Nice

This morning we went shopping in the hotel and bought some cute little ceramics. Then we returned to the beach where we saw an 82 year old lady gymnast who appeared to be about 65, the most. There were no wrinkles on her body which was amazing even when she removed her bra top and appeared half nude without any compunction whatsoever.

Off again—this time we drove to St. Paul De Vence, a medieval town in the mountains which was quite old and picturesque similar to Jaffa in Israel. There were also winding cobbled streets, and several artisan shops on each side with ceramics and furniture, etc. inside the various shops.

Then too there was a beautiful view and an abundant amount of flowers, including anemonies, mimosa and bougainvillia.

We had our lunch on the terrace of "La Residence" a cute little place in the square, overlooking the entire valley. What an experience and what a view!

We finally arrived back in Nice in time for a nap and to meet Armand Bousidan. He came promptly at 6:00 PM and took us to his "petite maison" which was gorgeous. It had a big square foyer with a marble floor. The walls were completely covered with a pale yellow brocade fabric and a table with a large porcelain flower in a beautiful vase was right in the center of the foyer. There was a long red silk bench to the left and on the right side there was a magnificent red fabric upholstered guest closet with gold and red silk hangers.

The living room was square also with a blue satin damask upholstered sofa, Ming dynasty vases, Louis 16th original chairs, 2 Louis 15th tables, a Chinese coffee table and marble pillars. There were also oriental rugs, a collection of old silver boxes and lovely paintings. It was all breathtaking! We also saw the dining room with a settee and two upholstered host and hostess chairs in gorgeous fabrics and finally the kitchen, completely tiled in Vallauris tiles with flowers. Everything was truly magnificent and certainly not a "petite maison".

Their daughter Michelle was 22 and most attractive but sophisticated. We only had champagne, cheese and nuts because the help was off. Then we went to dinner at St. Moritz with the Bousidans and it was great. We had cheese soufflé, paté de terrine, gigot (lamb), country string beans, squash and fried potatoes and finally a tart of apple and raspberries with whipped cream, all of which were simply wonderful. We took pictures and had a terrific time.

Afterwards we went to a discoteque with them. They were really so sweet. However the disco was dark, crowded and full of young kids. It was quite an experience and not to be forgotten! We finally walked through the old village of Nice and drove past their shop which was four stories high and most impressive.

Monday, October 21st—Nice

After due deliberation we decided not to go to St. Tropez but instead we went to La Reserve at Beaulieu. It was difficult to decide where to go in this area, but we finally checked out of the Negresco after having lunch at St. Moritz again. We had soufflé and apple tart, which was a repeat worth having. The help there welcomed us with a kiss on the hand and their little daughter Martine was most solicitous. After lunch we took a cab to Beaulieu.

We originally had misgivings upon our arrival at Beaulieu as the place is really quite small and it seemed to be extremely quiet and empty. However our room was lovely and the bathroom divine! The closet in the bedroom was like an armoire but it was built into the wall. It was black with nine panels of vased flowers all around like a garland, and with a Chippendale type of pediment on the top. It was absolutely beautiful. There was also a candlestick lamp on the dresser with a façade type shade which was most affective as well.

After walking around the town which appeared to be just a few streets, we stopped into a small café for a cup of tea, and finally returned to the hotel to dress for dinner. Al did not seem happy and I was not ecstatic either. However we had our dinner in the beautiful dining room, although the food was not that unusual. We had a mixed salad, good pea soup and a so so stuffed chicken leg on a bed of delicious spinach. There was no dessert.

After dinner we spent some time talking to a couple from Great Neck (Jewish) and then took a walk with them and another couple from Pittsburgh.

Herbert and Bea Flack from Great Neck and Ruth and Charles Lieber from Pittsburgh.

Tuesday, October 22nd—Beaulieu

Awakened this morning and the sun was so gorgeous, the air so clear and the flowers so aromatic and beautiful that we completely changed our minds and decided to stay in Beaulieu.

I had my hair done while Al sat at the pool with the Liebers and afterwards Al and I drove to Monaco on the lower corniche which was a beautifully scenic route along the Côte D'Azur. We found the town of Monaco to be unexciting, just little winding streets, a large courtyard, and the Palais which was being renovated.

We then continued to Monte Carlo. This seemed to be a fairly sizeable town, and a major part of it was, the Casino. We entered it and for fun I even put 2 coins in a machine. We then went to the hotel De Paris which we found to be luxuriously beautiful and apparently "the place to stay".

Cartiers was our next destination, where we saw a lovely bracelet that looked like a pavé tiger with black onyx spots. It was beautifully made and a pleasure to see.

We then drove to Eze village an artist colony in an old winding cobble roaded town high up on a mountain top. The view from there was spectacular and exhilarating and it was a really magnificent sight. The sky, mountains and sea below were breathtaking, and the clear pure air was special indeed.

The place was lined with intriguing little shops and studios and we walked into one which turned out to be that of the artist that the Bermans, Steiners and Diane Belfer have purchased paintings from—Doussard. However he was asking quite a lot for a small sized painting so we decided not to make a purchase.

We finally got back to Beaulieu where we befriended a butcher in an unusually lovely butcher shop furnished with beautiful French baker type racks on which he displayed his meats. They were old brass, iron, and marble and he told us that they had been in his family for over 100 years.

The Flacks joined us for dinner (it was just a salad and lots of hot vegetables and then some nice fruit and cake), but I was really distressed from so much eating. Again we walked through the town of Beaulieu with the Flacks who turned out to be good friends of Sybil Schneck. We were always meeting people who know each other. Europe seems to be a meeting place and we certainly feel very comfortable here.

Bedtime at last and we had only one more day of vacation. Tomorrow we leave this side of the world. Au Revoir!

October, 19th—Monte Carlo 1976

Here we were again embarked on a vacation in Europe. This time to revisit the French Riviera and looking forward to the delights of the Côte D'Azur with the Cedars.

We left New York at 10:30 PM via Air France and it was an uneventful trip on a 747. Luckily I managed to sleep a little before dinner arrived, which consisted of cold salmon with little peas and carrots in a sauce somewhat like mayonnaise, chicken breast stuffed with ham, accompanied by more peas, tiny onion, beets and chopped carrots that were marinated. There were also some wonderful cheeses and everything was délicieuse.

We arrived in Paris with just enough time to spare before catching the plane to Nice. But it was too bad that we had to miss the Free airport shopping.

From Nice we took a bus to Monte Carlo and enroute we passed Louis' Forum Beach and the Negresco Hotel, also La Reserve and these places all brought back fond memories of our last trip here.

The flowers were still blooming and it was a picturesque sight to see the vines trailing over the craggy rock formation on the walls along the way.

We arrived at The Hermitage Hotel which was old and quite charming. Our room was lovely and had very high ceilings. It also had Louis 16th moldings and over the doorways there were plaster relief designs. The walls themselves were pale pink with white moldings, and there was an olive green patterned rug and white art nouveau furniture including brass beds with brass footboards too. The bedspread was a pink floral stripe with olive green on white and everything in the room was upholstered in the same fabric. The lamp shades were shaped like an umbrella and had white silk fringe in scallops on the bottom. The bathroom had double sinks and a separate stall for the toilet and on the whole everything was extremely attractive.

After unpacking and resting, we then showered, dressed and went downstairs to have dinner. This proved to be a set menu with no selections at all but it was very good. We had a potato vegetable soup (thin), a sliced contra filet with little roast potatoes, string beans and caramel custard with bruillé sauce!

Since we were all weary we just walked around the town square for a while and then went to the Hôtel De Paris and spent some time in the casino (I lost $1.50 in the slot machine) which was just about the same amount I lost on my last visit. We finally went to bed and had a welcome night's sleep.

Saturday October 21st—Monte Carlo

Our room had a beautiful view of the harbor quite reminiscent of Haifa at night and it was a pleasure to awaken at 8:00 AM to witness a lovely day.

After breakfast we tried to rent a car to no avail, and so we had to take a bus into Nice, and when there we enjoyed the lovely sights along the water. We also walked along the street until we reached the Galerie Lafayette but unfortunately it was just in time for them to close for siesta, so we decided to have lunch at St. Moritz. As usual it was really delicious. We had salade niçoise, soufflé and the famous apple tart. The men had meringue glacé with chocolat, and everything was simply divine.

Then Phyllis and I did a little shopping for the children. We both spoke bad French but managed to be understood nevertheless.

We then met Al and Larry at Bouchera, the Bousidan's store and saw both of them there. We found out that Michelle was divorced (incidentally Al and I had been invited to her wedding but were not able to attend). The Bousidan's son was at the store also and he is very handsome. It was absolutely wonderful seeing them again as they are a most engaging couple and they kindly invited us to have dinner with them that evening but we had to make it for Wednesday night instead.

It was a little difficult conversing with them without Michelle to interpret, but we did find out that Armand had a recent cataract operation which apparently was successful.

After a little more shopping in Nice we went to La Reserve for cocktails and it was still a beautiful place. We soon returned to Monte Carlo and Phyllis and I visited a children's clothing shop where we both bought some lovely things for our grandchildren.

It was a long and tiring day so we were all happy to go to our rooms to rest before dinner.

Dinner itself consisted of consommé, etoiles, chicken with rice and meringué glacé. After dinner we went to the casino. This was really a fascinating place. We saw many turbaned Arabs gambling with large sums of money and other Europeans doing the same thing. They were all glued to their tremendous holdings and to the gambling tables as well. On the other hand, I just lost $2.00 in the slot machines. This seemed to be the extent of my gambling career as I personally found the gambling situation most unappealing. However all in all it was a fun day and we were all weary so thankfully it was now bedtime!

Sunday, October 22nd

We awakened at 9:30AM and were still tired. We had a good breakfast in our room and noticed that the day was magnificent, clear, and sunny. The water below our room was glistening in the sun and many boats were out rocking away in the blue water.

Al and I then decided to take a walk near the Hôtel De Paris and this was fun for a while as the day really promised to be continuously nice, but after an hour or so we realized it was almost time for our afternoon repast therefore we met the Cedars and went to the Piscine Des Terrasses which was lovely indeed. They were serving their famous Sunday brunch that consisted of grapefruit, hearts of palm salad, cold salmon with the usual little carrots and peas in that nice mayonnaise sauce. This seemed to be a specialty on the Côte D'Azur. Then we had a marvelous fish "Loupine" and it was absolutely divine. They also served a pot roast with vegetables and a pimento and ham omelet. Tarte tatin was the dessert (but not as good as the one at the St. Moritz). I must say we really stuffed ourselves which is not a good thing at all. Our vacations seem to be food extravaganzas and this will eventually lead to FAT!.

Off again to Menton for a drive along the beach. We even picked up some pebbles but they were not as pretty as the ones we previously found in Nice. The shops in Menton displayed beautiful candies however, and they were very colorful and in lovely shapes like fruit, flowers, Swiss cheese and even adorable little mice. They were all made of marzipan.

Then we went to the municipal Musée which was a disappointment. It seemed to be a real tourist trap.

Our drive back to Monte Carlo was most harrowing as we returned on the crowded Moyenne corniche. These corniches were extremely dangerous to say the least.

Finally we all had a drink at the Hôtel De Paris and took a rest before dinner.

Dinner time again and I don't think we will ever stop eating. This time we ate at our hotel and had pea soup, veal and strawberries Romanov.

Afterwards thankfully we took a much needed walk on the main shopping street near us. There were some nice things in the windows but most of them seemed to be junky. However it was fun, almost like walking on Worth Avenue at night.

This time we decided not to stay up too late as it will probably be a busy day tomorrow, Eze village etc.

Monday, October 23rd

In the morning we went to San Remo along the Menton Water Route and first stopped at the Menton town hall marriage bureau to see the decorations made by Jean Cocteau. They were lovely indeed and were symbolic of man's battle against women and also self destruction. They were painted like a maze.

When we reached San Remo we first entered a lovely children's clothing store that had gorgeous clothes and especially unusual sweaters but they were extremely expensive and not suitable for the 5 towns, so we bought rien!

On to Enrico's, the Pucci store, where everything was gorgeous. They had wonderful coats and suits, etc but were also very expensive. However we did buy a few things, pants for Nancy, a shirt and tie for Al and a dress for me.

Lunch time again! This time we went to the "Rendezvous" where we had risotto with parmesan cheese and mushrooms, my favorite, and it was extremely good. Al went out and bought his own raspberries and the waiter put gelati on top, It was delicieuse!

We then proceeded to Eze Village where Doussot had doubled his previous prices for even the smallest paintings and they were not such good ones either, so again we did not make a purchase.

We did however buy a nice little native dress for Lizzie in a cute baby shop.

Alas calamity struck—Al left the lights on in the car and we could not get it started. Luckily though a kind man came to our rescue and after much shoving and pushing, we got the darn thing going and were able to get back to our Hotel in time for a nap and bath.

Dinner there was a cheese pancake, chicken with string beans and rice pudding with fruit sauce.

We again walked on the avenue and then sat in the lobby with the Schepps (Sue Feldman) and Peggy Shacknow. They were lovely girls who knew Evelyn Wiley and Sylvia Leeds and as usual everybody in Europe knows everyone else in America.

Tuesday, October 24th

In the morning we drove to Cannes after a brief stop at the Negresco in Nice. It was still a lovely hotel and pleasant for us to revisit.

We then did a little shopping in the Courreges shop in Cannes where I bought two sweaters and tried on a gorgeous jacket. Unfortunately it was too small.

Then we went to the Blue Bar for lunch where we had a delicious salade niçoise, a mushroom omelet and a pudding with floating island sauce. All was most tasty! (Can these things possibly be fattening?)

At the next table we met a French couple who lived in Paris. He was in the men's clothing business (manufacturer) Jewish and very pleasant. We had a lovely conversation in half English and half French which was fun. After that we continued on to Vallauris and the Picasso Museé. His war and peace paintings were powerful indeed. We also picked up a lady in our car who was very tired and lived in Vallauris. She was really cute and could not believe that Phyllis was a grandmother. She said she had a great love for Americans particularly because she remembered that during the war (2nd world war) the American soldiers had distributed bon bons to the French children in her area. She was originally from North Africa but loved living in France.

On the way we passed an unusual motel "Marina Baie Des Anges" which was shaped like a sail boat on various levels and was quite different.

Eventually we reached the Leger Museé that was a gorgeous building with fantastic paintings by Leger in all different mediums, ceramic, stained glass, and oils, plus magnificent rugs, and it was a spectacular monument to a great artist. We also bought a lovely stamped litho for Kenny and Barbi.

We then drove to Vence and the Maeght Foundation Musée. This was a most exciting building to behold. Each artist was represented in a special garden setting with sculptures outdoors. There were Miros, Braques, Giacometti's, Chagall's, Kandinsky's, etc. I bought a Chagall poster which I loved! It was an exceptional day, and to be able to witness such magnificent modern art was awesome!

We finally drove back to Monte Carlo at dusk and decided to just have a drink and not change for dinner. This consisted of tomato bisque, grilled veal and potato puffs. There was a peculiar dessert that I did not eat. It was something like ice cream but not entirely. Anyway after such a wearying day we were happy to go to bed.

Wednesday, October 25th

This morning we had to go to Nataly's kiddie shop to exchange Lizzie's dress for another size and then we continued on to a men's shop for a hat that Al wanted.

We started eating again! This time we had lunch with Phyllis and Larry at Rompaldi's and we had spaghetti carbonera, salade niçoise and raspberries. It was a pleasant afternoon but we barely had time to shower, dress and leave for dinner in Nice with the Bousidans.

We arrived in Nice and first went to Vuitton to buy a briefcase for Mark. Luckily Vuitton was right next to the provincial fabric shop, where they had adorable robes and bags, etc. all in the same provincial type fabrics as the bag I bought on my last trip to the Riveria.

Then we continued on to the Bouchera store to meet Gilberte and Armand. Gilberte looked lovely in what she termed a "costume" (pantsuit). It was black velvet and white satin and she looked most attractive, of course being so pretty helped her appearance.

We then went to a cute little bar in the Hotel Plaza the "Crazy" where we all had a great drink called "Paradise". It was gin, orange juice, grenadine, and had a sugared rim on the glass. There was also a bit of lemon too. Gilberte had invented this drink.

We then had to call Michelle to join us as it was difficult for us to talk to the Bousidans easily. So we went to the restaurant Le Chaumière which was an adorable place in Ville Franche and where they cook everything on their grille. Michelle met us there with a lovely young man Lucien A Bio. He was a chemist and charming.

It really was a wonderful evening and we enjoyed marvelous grilled steak and lamb, sliced marinated red peppers, saladé in a sweet cream sauce with onions pepper and vinegar, tomatoes, celery and radishes.

During dinner Armand peeled an artichoke for me down to the heart. Then he put onion and vinegar and oil on it! It was absolutely delicious. We also had toasted bread and butter with red peppers on it. The first course was melon with proscuito ham and paté de fois de canard next. We also had plenty of wine and a green salad with oil and vinegar. Everything was superb. Our dessert was tarte tatin with raspberries on the side including heavy whipped cream—Great! (But we were all exploding).

We then sent a postcard to the Perlmans from the restaurant explaining how much we missed them.

Confidentially the Bousidans told us that they were unhappy because Michelle is not married. Her young man is poor and has an uncertain future in chemistry so they were not anxious for her to marry him.

They insisted upon treating us to this dinner which was really so kind of them and it truly was a wonderful evening and the highlight of our trip. We kissed them goodbye and left with hopes that we would return someday. They also invited us to come to Nice in September as they have a boat and we will be welcome to sail with them for a few days. They really could not have been more gracious.

Thursday, October 26th

We decided to go to the Rothchild Museé at St. Jean Cap Ferrat today which was the home of Madame Ephruiseé, a daughter of the Rothchilds. There was a gorgeous view and her possessions were wonderful.

After that we returned to Beaulieu for lunch at a little pizza place where we just had salade, pizza, and chocolate roll.

On our way back to Monte Carlo we stopped at Givenchy where Al bought a pretty tie and I bought an unusual belt. There is nothing as great as shopping in France—Ooh La La!

That night we had dinner with the Schepps, the Schachman's, and Phyllis and Larry at Au Bec Rouge. This was marvelous food indeed. We had Feuilltage De Morelles in pastry shells with huge mushrooms that was then baked in a large shell like puff. Then we had chicken cordon bleu (ham and swiss cheese fried crisp), french fries and chocolate cream filled puffs (milk chocolate and divine) for dessert. There were tiny country radishes with big leaves on the table, a guitar player sang and all in all it was a lovely evening and a charming way to end our vacation, fattening as it was.

Friday, October 27th

I had my hair done at 9:00 AM and then went back to Hermes to send a scarf to Gilberte. Unfortunately it started to rain and the plane trip to Paris was uneventful but we were able to have a little time to shop in the airport in Paris for a few sundries and gifts before the flight time to New York was announced.

However in the 747 on the way home we had an unpleasant experience. There was a mix up in the sale of space on the plane and a few people had duplicate seats.

A couple named Benjamin from the Tam-O-Shanter Club refused to sit elsewhere and for one hour the flight was delayed.

Finally after a passenger swore profusely at them they conceded, whereas previously the whole Air France staff as well as the police could not persuade them to change their seats willingly. They just wanted to sit together. Everyone thought they were stupid and unfeeling.

However we arrived home safely and Kenny met us. Thank Heavens all was well at home. Our vacation was now over and everyone agreed that it was a wonderful trip. Au Revoir again!

October 19th, 1977
Hotel Torme Normana—Alta Villa—Palermo, Italy

Upon Starting this trip we had many misgivings as the Glickman's and Landi's cancelled and of course this was a huge disappointment.

However we nevertheless approached the airport with a feeling of jubilation and with hopeful vacation spirits. These feelings unfortunately were soon to be dispelled as no one at the airport was particularly attractive. There were mostly Italians visiting their homeland and also a very jazzy group who were seeking an inexpensive vacation at a group airfare. We finally took off at 9:30 AM but had to stop in Boston for some reason as our actual departure became 1 AM.

Luckily we had bulkhead seats next to a Dentist and his wife from Poughkeepsie. We also met a cute DDS and his wife from New Jersey. Paul Markowitz and Germaine. They were young but friendly and most pleasant.

Nothing exciting happened during the flight except that we managed to see the Alps all snow covered in the early morning, which was a treat.

Thursday, October 20th—Airport—Palermo

At last we arrived in Palermo at 1:45 PM and it was a lovely day. There were beautiful mountains on one side and the Mediterranean on the other. However it was quite arid and brown so we abandoned the idea of driving to the hotel and took the bus which was a one and half hour trip.

The terrain was quite mountainous with lots of Bouganvillia, big fat cactus plants and olive trees along the way. There were also many modern residential areas en route with dark blue or green or orange shutter blinds on the windows of the small houses.

We ultimately passed a cute watermelon wagon all painted in an unusual way and then saw a little band of children playing various home made instruments—pans, tin cans, harmonicas, and other metal pieces. They were a gay and happy bunch who danced as well (apparently they were intent on entertaining us).

There were quite a lot of winding roads, some hair pin curves and finally the mountainous area of Torme Normana which was much like Doral. There were rooms setup in buildings strewn around the central building and the whole place appeared to be quite rustic.

A nice gesture was a little welcome band with signs greeting us. They played the March from Aida (which happened to be my graduation march from high school) and there was wine, popcorn and other tidbits being served around the pool. The place itself was fairly attractive but the rooms were so so. In our room the floors were navy blue tile, there was a cranberry colored desk and chairs with rush seats in the same color, white formica night stands with cranberry trim and white porcelain lamps. A veranda with chairs were in each room but the shower was rather small.

Then after we opened our luggage, a man next door to us called from his terrace and asked if we could open his door as he was locked in. This was calamity #1.

We finally dressed for dinner and then a further disappointment set-in. At 6:30 PM we tried to make a reservation at the Taormina San Domenica but were unable to do so as the desk help were most difficult and then we could not find the restaurant, and we could not find the pizza place either. So we wandered aimlessly about looking for the reception desk to no avail. Finally at about 8:00 PM we found the restaurant and had dinner with the Markowitz's and just had soup, macaroni and wine.

From 9 to 10 Pm we wandered around again looking for our room, intermittingly meeting other people looking for their rooms or their luggage or the restaurant and we became absolutely hysterical laughing as it was such a farce. (Hopefully tomorrow will be better).

Friday, October 21st, Palermo and Monreale

We went outside our cabin and this time we found the dining room easily (daylight is surely a big help). Everything there was served buffet style and breakfast consisted only of big fat rolls and tea. If you ordered juice there was an extra charge and nothing else there was particularly inviting.

We then got on the hotel bus in order to take the city tour. Luckily we met a lovely couple, Fred and Dede Rubin from Old Westbury. He was an attorney and she was a psychologist and we went with them to the cathedral which was entirely covered by mosaics which were mostly gold, and there was a cedar wood ceiling in a Moroccan style, and the entire place was really a remarkable sight.

Then we visited the four corners in the city depicting the four seasons of the year, and in the garden of the church we saw a plant which had leaves that if you touched them they would curl up, then not open again for a few hours.

We couldn't help noticing how bustling the city was on a work day but everybody appeared poor and there were just a few interesting shops on the one good street in town.

Afterwards we stopped at a little bar for a cheese sandwich on a roll. Then Al opted out of going to Monreale and we were unable to give away our tickets. Instead we returned to the hotel and sat around the pool with Germaine Markowitz. She really was a darling girl who used to teach French in Lubbock, Texas.

Al and I then went for a drive to Trabani, a little hill town where all the people sat out in the street, along which there were little stalls displaying many kinds of typical Sicilian items. Another little town had a small street where the women sat in their doorways, facing the doorways and knitting and crocheting. They all had their laundry hanging out and had cotton curtains covering their doors. Apparently everyone there was very poor.

After we returned to our hotel we went out to dinner with the Rubins to a little place called Pietros where we had delicious pasta rigatoni with tomatoes, anchovies, oregano and garlic, and thankfully Fred drove. We all had veal cutlets with mushrooms and then cassata for dessert. This was a very rich cake with candied fruit. It was a really great dinner with much vino and included a lot of fun with the Rubins. The waiter was extremely pleasant and the entire dinner cost $25 for four people including two bottles of vino. Maybe we should think about moving there!!

When we got back to the hotel we made arrangements to go to Agrigento with the Rubins the next day and to Taorimina at the Hotel Timeo on Sunday.

Saturday, October 22nd—Agrigento

We awakened to a beautiful morning, a clear and cool day with dry mountain air. The mountains were almost like an elephant hide in color and texture and they were right outside the restaurant area, so it was like seeing an animal in the distance.

We met the Rubins for breakfast which was just the usual roll and tea, and then we drove to Agrigento on the Auto Strada, a two and one half hour trip through beautiful mountain areas, terraced hills, vineyards, olive trees and persimmon trees all on a beige, taupe, olivey toned terrain, as well as wide vistas of land, mountains and sky.

Then we finally reached the Temple of Concord in Agrigento which proved to be remarkably preserved ruins similar to the Athena in Greece, only this place had a peanut colored, old spongy texture to the Doric columns that supported the temple and also the ruins. It all dated back to about 700 BC.

We then picked up several stones on the ground which appeared to have shells from the sea embedded in them. This seemed to be an unusual situation as we were so high up in altitude. Either the stones were transported from sea level or the whole place was under water at one time. At any rate it was fascinating and wonderful to witness such a remarkably preserved sight.

Since it apparently was close to lunch time we went to a little restaurant recommended by the postcard truck man. It looked pretty awful so we left there and went to the Hotel Villa Athena instead. This proved to be positively delightful. We even looked at the rooms, which were all beautiful and each room had a terrace leading to the pool, with trumpet bells and bougainvillea cascading down the steps. In fact it would have been great to have stayed there had we known it existed.

After some excellent local wine on the terrace we proceeded to have a wonderful lunch. We had antipasto of various eggplant, pepper and bean dishes and ziti pasta with tomato and eggplant. It truly was a perfect day.

Then came the long trip back to Torme Normana where we took a much needed nap until 5 PM, at which time we went with our new best friends (the Rubins) to Cefalu. This was a quaint, bustling, narrow streeted little town on the side of the mountain coasted by the Mediterranean, and there were little seafood restaurants with red gingham checked table cloths all along the street.

We then happened upon a ceramic shop which had wonderful spaghetti dinnerware in delightful colors so of course we had to buy them.

Luckily the owner of the shop took us in his car to a very good restaurant where we had tasty veal, more pasta and more vino. It was really nice of him to escort us there but he probably got a kickback for doing so. At any rate it was a nice way to end a long but fun day and we were all extremely weary. Bedtime ho hum!

Sunday, October 23rd—Weather beautiful

Awakened to another glorious day, it was crystal clear with almost an echo in the air and I have to say the mountains truly were a lovely sight to behold. At any rate we had our breakfast and then got ready for our next trip, which was to Taormina.

John the taxi driver helped Al move the car and load our luggage and then told Al he was a very nice man and that he liked him better than any of the other people on the trip. He was probably right to feel that way.

We then got on the Auto Strada and drove through magnificent hills and a steep mountainous terrain. It had soft beige, yellow, greenish olive tones and was sparsely shrubbed. The earth was dark and only occasionally cultivated. It was almost like being totally alone in the world. There were few cars on the road and the sunshine was dazzling. I must admit that Mussolini did one good thing as the roads were great which made for easy driving.

We finally got to Catania where we had anticipated having lunch at a famous restaurant but what a fiasco that was! It turned out that the city was the craziest place. Cars were going every which way plus there were no city street lights, hordes of wild people, and lots of pushcarts that were on every corner selling nuts, round loaves of bread, long red radishes, finuchi, cabbage, wine and shoes etc! It was a marketplace beyond compare. The little winding streets were no wider than our Fiat and the traffic was going two ways no less. Al was a wreck, he perspired in streams and I was frightened and not happy. No one spoke English and we could not find our way out of that awful mess. After circling the same terrible dark, dingy old streets several times, we finally came to a fairly new area where it seemed safe to stop to eat a piece of cake and have some tea while we were standing up, and then we forgot completely about that fancy restaurant we originally had in mind.

Thankfully after a policeman stopped us and told us to get out of town quickly before we got hurt, we were touted onto the correct road to Massina, which proved to be the newer and better section of Cantania. Along that road there were lovely apartment houses and some nice private homes.

Then we continued on towards Taormina and got off at Taormina "Sud" which was a mistake. This proved to be the lower city and was right on the water with all the lesser quality hotels. Even the "Mazzara Sea Palace" which had been recommended by the clerk at the Torme Normana was not what we considered to be suitable.

Finally though we made the correct turn and started driving up an extremely high mountain and soon found ourselves going around frightening bends and curves on stilted supports and at times I thought Al would have apoplexy.

At last however we got to the village of Taormina which had narrow, quaint little streets lined with boutiques and cafes. It appeared to be quite old and looked almost like a toy town. Unfortunately we then took the wrong turn and missed finding our hotel and stalled the car as well.

Finally good fortune prevailed and we were able to locate our hotel. Guess what . . . it was positively charming! It was densely shrubbed with a flowered courtyard entrance. A gracious clerk was there and the charming interior made us feel welcome. We were taken to our room which was in a corner with 2 balconies lined with flowers and cascading vines, plus it had a view of Mt. Etna smoking in the distance. It was paradise at last! We were also able to see the curved harbor in the forefront and the lovely village to the right. The other side of the balcony faced the gardens, other terraces and an old mountain with ancient ruins on top. Also people were walking all around below us. It was truly a magnificent sight. As Al said it was worth the trip otherwise he was prepared to kill me!

For quite some time we sat outside luxuriating in the beautiful scene before us and enjoyed breathing in the soft and balmy air.

Then after a while we decided to walk down the hill to the main part of town, and strolled along the shopping area. It was kind of like an Italian Worth Avenue but very narrow.

There were lots of people meandering about but the merchandise displayed in the shops was not particularly attractive and it consisted mainly of bric a brac and souvenirs so I don't believe the people walking were making any purchases.

There was, however some exceedingly beautiful candy in various fruit shapes almost like works of art in one shop but I don't know if they tasted as great as they looked.

There were many cafes in the area, an occasional wildly decorated donkey cart and one shop with nice sweaters and embroidered shirts but not much else.

Nevertheless it was nice to get a feel of the town and then we returned to the Hotel to rest until dinner time.

Our next activity was drink time in the lovely living room type bar after which we proceeded to the dining room where everything was beautifully served. We had rigatoni (tomato, garlic, lots of pepper and cheese) then a grilled veal chop, string beans, french fries (delicious!), salad, cheese, and 3 baked pears with a cherry in each of them. Tea was served in the bar. It was quite continental and good, plus it certainly dispelled the gaucherie of the Torme Normana cuisine.

All in all it was the most pleasant day of this trip so far. You might say it was complete luxury in a European fashion.

Monday, October 24th—Taormina

We awakened to witness a beautiful morning again and wanted to thank the weather man for delivering a lovely day, as such loveliness is certainly in our favor. Mt. Etna was not smoking quite as much as yesterday but the sight of it was most impressive.

All the houses on the Hillside were rust colored, white and with a touch of green. The poplar trees were profusely clumped and stood erect, and olive trees, bougainvillea and orange and lemon trees were lovely to see. However there always seemed to be a mist over the mountains.

We had breakfast on the outside terrace and had rolls, jam and English tea. Al had coddled eggs in an egg cup which he said were very good.

After breakfast we strolled down Umberto Street and bought a few knick knacks and then went to San Domenico where we made a reservation for dinner on Tuesday. I was rather glad we were staying at the Timeo as it is more intimate and gracious.

Then we returned to our hotel for a while until it was again time to have lunch. Food is all we seemed to think about and it was really becoming an obsession. Our choice for lunch this time was in a delightful little outdoor terrace café called La Bucca. We had risotto and mushrooms and cheese, plus pears and vino.

Just as we finished eating, the Rubins came by looking for us and we spent the rest of the day with them, again strolling down Umberto Street and making nice little purchases en route. Nothing was really outstanding but of course it is fun to have things to remember Taormina. Ultimately we returned to our hotel, having met several of the couples from our tour on our way back. All of them said they have been enjoying themselves as much as we have been.

We rested before dinner and then met the Rubins at our hotel for drinks at the bar. They mentioned woefully that they had a hair raising experience on the hill coming up to join us, as their car kept sliding back down the hill just as our car did when we arrived in Taormina. Nevertheless they were ready for dinner and we all had rissole with meat sauce and baby grilled lamp chops, broccoli and potatoes, salad, apple tart as well as corvo (a white Bordeaux which was a delicious wine with a fruity flavor and a slight bubbly taste). This was even better then the Dracena Bordeaux we had on other occasions. I do believe the Rubins enjoyed the dinner at the Timeo as opposed to the meals at their hotel.

After dinner we watched the coastline below us and the twinkly lights we saw looked almost like a Christmas tree with all the bulbs flickering.

Al and I really felt that this was a true vacation day. In fact we decided not to visit Mt. Etna tomorrow as it might be too much of a hassle and the memory of today was sufficient.

Tuesday, October 25th, Taormina—Gorgeous Weather

This morning (just like all the others have been) was simply perfect. It was clear and the temperature could not have been improved upon.

We had our usual breakfast on the terrace and this time all the tables were covered with lovely blue or yellow cloths. We both had very tart juice, boiled eggs in an egg cup and tea.

The bees were buzzing around but they did not sting which was most kind of them.

After our leisurely morning food intake we went for a most delightful walk in the garden below the terrace. What a wonderful experience that was! Every conceivable flower was displayed in profusion. Clumps of nastursiums, yellow carnations, roses, bougainvillia, clover in a deep red, some lavender blossoms, yellow oranges and spiking cacti all growing together under archways of leaves. Also there were terraces filled with pots of geraniums and other flowers I never saw before and as far as the eye could see. They seemed to go on and on and included asters and zinnias as well.

The Timeo was indeed a lovely hotel with plenty of old world charm and intimacy. I was so happy we did not go to San Dominico.

After that wonderful experience in the gardens we took another stroll in town and tried to complete our list of gift purchases. It was really difficult to find anything appropriate however.

Finally we returned to the Timeo for lunch and saw "Rocco" impeccably turned out as the typical Maître D'. The napkins on the tables were crisply starched to the breaking point and the menu was most appealing. We had little short cut noodles with ham, tomato and cheese, then a divine grilled local fish with caponata, sliced cheese and fruit salad. We had tea with Ann and Joe Berkman from Mamaroneck (she was very cute) and then went to Castle Male on top of the mountain, which became a harrowing and frightening experience. There were many round impassable curves, the road went straight up and was constantly winding, our ears started popping and the air was rarified. However we finally reached the top and discovered a quaint little town which was quite small and appeared to be less Honky Tonk than Taormina's shopping street. An awesome experience greeted us when we finally climbed to the very top which towered above all the hills of Taormina. It was an unbelievable sight. After peering around for a brief time, we made the hazardous trip down and then visited the Greek amphitheatre next to our hotel. This was huge and in fairly good repair so far as ruins are concerned.

After a short rest time we dressed for dinner which we were slated to have at the San Domenico with the Rubins, however when we got there Fred said he didn't think we should eat there as it was almost deserted and the menu did not look so good. He happened to be right as the menu really looked awful, so after walking around their hotel for a while I came to the conclusion that being at the Timeo was the much better choice. The San Domenico had been a nun's convent at one time and the doors to the rooms were all so low you had to duck your head in order to enter them. Also the halls were wide and long and were unattractive as well. Nevertheless the one redeeming feature was the glass enclosed courtyard which had a huge Bouganvilla in the center.

We finally decided to have dinner with the Rubins at La Chicops which was not a good choice. The pasta (green and white with tomatoes and cheese) was cold and the scampi was grilled but not split and were also cold. The custard dessert was just so so, therefore we decided to go to a nearby outdoor café for tea. Happily the Rubins are really lovely people and it has been a pleasure being with them. They certainly helped to make this vacation a success.

After taking a taxi back to our hotel we tried to organize our belongings for the return to "Torme Terrible" as Ann Berkman called it. (Oh dear I can't seem to find my used roll of film. I hope it is not lost forever.)

Wednesday, October 26th—Weather

Great As Usual

Again awakened in the early morning to the ringing of the local church bells in a slow, then staccato manner which lasted until 7:00 Am when we had to get up.

We finished our packing and then went down to the terrace for a final breakfast at the Timeo and we were told the waiter was really sorry we missed having dinner there last evening. I am sure it would have been a wonderful repast as he named the great items that had been on the menu and they certainly sounded enticing. Joe Berkman joined us for breakfast as Ann had (as she put it—Garibaldi's revenge).

Everything was served in its usual gracious manner, and the surroundings were extremely peaceful with the birds twittering, in addition to the aromatic scent of the beautiful flowering shrubs. Even the bees kept their distance and did not buzz around our rolls and tea. We will definitely miss these lovely days at the Timeo and thankfully we will have wonderful memories.

When we walked down to Umberto Street to get the paper, we learned that Palermo had a riot yesterday caused by the communist forces who were up in arms against the massasacre of the hi-jackers of a German airliner last week. I'm sure glad we missed that episode.

The smoke coming from Mt. Etna was going in the opposite direction this morning and the haze was starting to envelop the entire mountainside down to the coast. Nature is really incredible and one never knows what will happen next.

Every so often we have seen a little old lady feeding the cats in the courtyard and just found out that she is the owner of the Timeo. She seems to be at least 85 so apparently her father or grand father built the hotel as it is purported to be over 200 years old.

We then made plans to leave here at noon and decided to follow the Rubins out of town as they seem to be good navigators and Al and I are definitely not in that category.

Therefore we picked them up at the San Domineco and followed them smoothly through to Catania. This time we had no mishaps and then we drove through the same arid elephant colored and textured hills and mountains. There was hardly any cultivation except a few orange groves and some olive trees, to be seen, so it was a fairly dismal ride.

All the little towns and isolated old houses faded into the same dim colored hills. No doubt they were built with the rocks and stones found in the area.

At last we arrived at "Torme terrible" just in time to learn that our flight home would leave at 11:00 PM from the hotel and at 2:00 AM from the airport, so we had just another day before we would arrive home in America, and hopefully this would be at a more reasonable hour.

For dinner we went to a terrible little restaurant nearby, where we had pizza, spaghetti and lemon ice, (actually it was not dreadful, not awful, just bad!)

Again we had to organize our luggage and decided to forego watching the Sicilian dance group that had been scheduled to perform on this last evening of the trip, although we did catch a glimpse of the troupe, which seemed to be all children in native regalia. They wore lovely hand crocheted aprons over their costumes. However we were really tired and opted for bed—yawn, yawn, yawn!

Thursday October 27th—Tormé Normana

Today it is a little cooler than it was in Taormina, but still rather lovely. It was just shirt and sweater attire.

We had breakfast with the Rubins and we decided to return to Cefalu since we really never saw it in the day time. This time we were able to park right in front of the ceramic shop and thought we should buy that De Simone lithograph we had admired on our previous visit, so we did and our new friend the owner gave us a slight discount. Then Didi bought more dishes to complete her set. After we finalized our transactions we strolled down the quaint little crooked streets and then made a few other purchases including a lovely pair of boots for me. Cefalu is really a bustling happy town with nice people and it was a lovely experience to visit it.

Since we were not quite hungry we decided to have a picnic lunch in the town square in front of the cathedral, where they had little tables and chairs set out café style. The men then bought cheese, wonderful crusty rolls, home baked cookies and fresh persimmons. They also bought a bottle of Corvo and Dracena so we had a splendid feast and everyone around us was jealous. We had to borrow a knife to cut the rolls and the owner of the store where they were bought, personally came out to open the wine which came from his sister-in law's shop. He had originally taken Al and Fred there to purchase the bottles. He was a very nice man and we had a fun luncheon. It was much better than if we had eaten in a restaurant.

After "our feast" we drove to Cacama, a hill town near Trabia. When we started driving up the mountain we did not realize the distance or the incline so for 20 minutes we climbed and climbed, steeper and steeper until our ears popped on those narrow curved roads and both Didi and I were frightened and apprehensive.

Finally! Thank the good lord, we reached this little town high in the hills which looked down onto the lower part of the mountain that greatly resembled the Grand Canyon. It had crazy, winding steep streets, cars every which way and we were all nervous. At last! We reached the top only to find that it was solely inhabited by elderly priests. One man sat on a bench (armless) backwards, on the edge of the mountain. It was an extremely frightening sight. I was sure he was going to topple over into oblivion.

Then another man came by and we could tell he thought we were insane to be there in a car since nobody else ever did so. No wonder the road was so empty.

The only other live beings seemed to be chickens just clucking and roaming around.

Ultimately another man came out of the facility and told us in broken English and no teeth that he used to live in Morristown New Jersey. "whaddia know"! Maybe he was a displaced American.

Going back down was not as bad as going up but we were all most happy to finally reach Trabia and get back to the hotel to change for dinner, which we had at Al Nepale. Thankfully the pasta was good and we also had grilled fish and once again had persimmons and apples.

When we turned in the car at the reception desk we found out that our trip would be delayed until 5:00 AM in the morning so we tried to get some sleep until then.

Hopefully we expected to arrive in New York around 1:00 PM on Friday.

Finally we left Tormé Normana at 4:00 AM but unfortunately a delay at the airport was caused by a man who supposedly had a heart attack and was not permitted to board the plane without a doctor's sanction.

This sadly caused us to lose our slot in London therefore we finally left at 8:30 AM on World Airways.

At any rate we arrived at Gatwick Airport in London and we were able to stay there for 2 hours, so we had lunch and did some more shopping.

When we got back to the plane we were served a wonderful lunch (but that was 2 hours later). Everything was beautifully prepared however, and consisted of good chicken, nice fresh vegetables, salad and a lovely warm Danish and tea.

Boston was the next stop where we could see the beautiful fall leaf tones from the air in their truly glorious glowing colors. Yellow, red, russet and green. Thank heavens we cleared customs safely, bid farewell to Fred and Didi, and we were sincerely hoping to see them again soon.

At last we got back on our plane and proceeded to Kennedy Airport. Everything seemed fine until the last 10 minutes when we dipped sharply and everyone's ears practically exploded until we finally touched ground. Oh how great it was to be back on home soil after a wondrous vacation! Ciao!

Sunday, November 4th, 1978—Paris Again

Al and I left New York for the airport with Nancy who drove us at 8:00 PM, only to find that our flight was scheduled to be delayed for 2 hours. This was not a pleasant prospect but Al being as enterprising as ever walked into the 1st class waiting salon and we stayed there illegally until it was time to board the plane.

While there we met a very charming young German attorney who had been traveling around the world for the past 6 weeks. He was extremely bright and pleasant, nevertheless I couldn't help equating him with a Nazi background.

The salon also was filled with fashion people enroute to the fall shows in Paris, and several black Africans going to Dakar with lots of their children who were all speaking French, and dressed in their native attire. They all seemed to be intelligent and affluent.

We finally boarded the plane and luckily were placed in the bulkhead seats we had requested so at least we hoped to be comfortable.

I must say they really do things right on Air France as we were served a truly beautiful and delicious dinner. There were slivers of beets and celery hearts in a delightful sauce, poached salmon, sliced egg and the usual French peas and mayonnaise salad. Then we had creamed chicken, rice and mushrooms, cheese, French bread and pastry (although that was too sweet) and of course lots of wine was served with our dinner.

Then before we knew it they started serving breakfast so we had juice, Danish and tea. Shortly after that we arrived in Paris which was 12:00 noon their time and thankfully the Hotel California sent a car to meet us and then drove us to the hotel. While still at the airport though we met Martha Levine and her daughter Lynn. They were on a buying trip for clothes intended for their Palm Beach shop. Martha is still quite strange and snobbish and referred to me as "Brookov's daughter".

The drive to the hotel was uneventful but it was terrific seeing all the familiar Parisian landmarks again. It was a beautiful day weather wise and I noticed many new apartment houses along the way and lovely poplar trees lining the road.

At last we arrived at the California which was a quite small but very pleasant hotel wonderfully situated right off the Champs Elyseé.

Our room was lovely and had a working fireplace. There was also a large bathroom and an enormous armoire.

After a necessary nap we left the hotel and took a leisurely walk along the Champs Elyseé. We were really thrilled to be back in Paris and chanced upon a chestnut man so of course we bought some. They were delicious, hot, plump and sweet! The ones in New York are much smaller, and definitely not as good.

Since it was a Sunday, the streets were jammed with Parisians out strolling and many of the ladies wore leopard coats. These days that is an unusual sight because America will not allow the leopard skins to enter our ports. Apparently this ruling does not apply in France.

We were happy to notice that the Champs Elyseé was just as exciting as ever and we really enjoyed eying the many attractive shop windows with their lovely contents. We also bought "crèpes avec marrons" from a pushcart and then more roasted chestnuts. I guess we are victims of La gastronomie.

Since it started becoming a little brisk and blowey we decided to return to the hotel, and enroute we met two men from

Pennsylvania on the street, who recommended a restaurant for dinner.

So after a little nap we tried to go to that restaurant however it was closed on Sundays therefore we took our concierge's suggestion instead. This was "Ramponneau" and was really great. We had a lovely green salad, filet of sole in a fantastic sauce (mushrooms in cream), crusty rolls with butter curls and raspberries and whipped cream for dessert.

We also befriended the people at the next table who were from Columbia South America and knew the men Al does business with in New York. Coincidences always seem to crop up in Europe, which is truly amazing because this is such a big world.

After dinner our walking continued until we finally passed the Prince De Galles Hotel and called Jewel Garlick to inquire after Lou. He apparently is leaving the hospital tomorrow after having a bad heart attack.

We again continued along the Champs Elyseé but then stopped in for tea at a little sidewalk café before we returned to our hotel for a much needed night's sleep.

Monday, November 6th

Thank goodness we both slept well and awakened to a lovely crisp morning. "Le Petit Dejeuner" arrived with a crunchy roll, a croissant, a brioche, hot chocolat, and jam suffit.

After dressing we again went out for a walk. This time we went to the City Bank for some money and then took a taxi to Laurentious. The old man who previously owned the place apparently died this year and the ties were not as attractive as they formally were. However Al bought 6 of them and then we walked past the Galerie Layfayette where Al could not find "La Toilette". It was almost a calamitous situation. At any rate after solving that problem we bought Lizzie a jumper and then had lunch at a sidewalk bistro on Rue de Madelaine. We both had onion soup gratinée and Al had an omelette with mushrooms.

Again we continued our walk until we passed Rodier where I saw a very attractive green turtleneck dress in the window, so naturally I went in and bought it. Then we walked along Rue St. Honoré but the prices had become exhorbitant and it seemed impossible to make a purchase.

Subsequently we arrived back at our hotel after first stopping for a delicious mocha éclair at a patisserie that had all kinds of fancy shaped bread, like birds, chicken and fish, etc.

Dinner time again! This time we went to Raffatin and Honoré on the left bank which Hal Lipper had recommended. I had hors d'oeuves and duck a l'orange which was not the best. Al had salmon in cream sauce, but all in all it was a disappointing dinner, although the owner gave me a beautiful rose. We did meet some Americans there from Florida who suggested a restaurant named "Sherwood" near Harry's Bar.

However everyone has different taste so we decided to skip that one, although we may try Audil that our Columbian friends suggested.

Before returning to our hotel we stopped at Fouquets for a pastry and tea and also made friends with the waiter. He kindly invited us to return tomorrow night for a "cadeau".

Finally we returned to the California at 11 PM, after a long and fun day during which we really walked. Al thinks we traversed about 10 miles and I believe he was right! Good Night!

Tuesday, November 7th

Today we expect to go to one of Al's jewelers and peut être "Sagil" and "Michael Swisse". We both had a wonderful night's sleep and perhaps it was due to the lovely comforter (which was tufted in the shape of a criss cross button design) that made us sleep so well. There was also an unusual clock in our room where the face's voice announced the correct time. Our breakfast arrived and again was very good. The roll particularly was delish!

After reading the paper for a while we took a walk down Rue De Monteau which was parallel to the Champs Elyseé. This street has neighborhood type stores including beauty salons, food stuffs, moderate priced clothing, bars and patisseries. It was a very pleasant way to see Paris au pied and it was really marvelous the way they displayed food, which was arranged in such a picturesque manner (and the pastries as well!!) All these were unusually placed in the window and display cases.

Then we walked all the way to Rue St. Anne near the Place De L'Opera en route to one of Al's jewelers. Unfortunately he was out (after we had walked up 3 flights of stairs!).

Finally we walked to Rue De Capucine for lunch. It was not as good as yesterday even though we had the same onion soup (but it had less gratinée). Then we tried the Café de la Paix. But they only served dejeuner complêt. We were not interested in that so we continued our trekking along the Place Vendome and saw some fantastic jewels. There was a magnificent emerald and diamond (pear shape) necklace which Al thought cost about $1,000,000.000. We also saw some interesting rings. They had open shanks in the front and were set with many different colored stones. Most of the other necklaces seemed to have long open hanging drops.

After gazing at those wonderful items we went to Michael Swisse who is Branca's Brother, where we bought cosmetics.

The clothing prices here were really prohibitive although I saw a beautiful belt which I may buy if I can find the shop again. But we were tired by this time, so we walked back to our hotel to have a little nap and then went to Chez Michel for dinner, which was recommended by Marshall Tulin. It was a small bistro near the Gare Nord and when we got there it was quite empty but soon afterwards it filled up completely. Parisians do eat late. We had salad niçoise first, then they served olives, mushrooms with peppercorns and wonderful pâte a choux rolls with fromage on top—trés delicieuse!

Al had steak with béarnaise sauce for his main course and I had a lamb noisette with spinach roulade and a tomato slice on top plus truffles on the lamb. There were wonderful French fries as well. For dessert we both had soufflé grand marnier and feuilletté with framboise—merveiléuse. It was a wonderful dinner beautifully prepared by charming people as well.

Taxis however were hard to come by but we finally were able to get one which took us back to the Champs Elyseé where we bought our usual chestnuts and then walked back to our hotel and went to bed.

Wednesday, November 8th

We slept late until 9:30 AM in fact and then had our breakfast which was the usual croissants, tea and jam (I think I'm gaining weight minute by minute). We also had to go to the bank again as money disappears so quickly in Paris. Luckily though the air is really lovely and balmier than yesterday so it seemed to be a perfect day to go to Beaubourg. (The Pompideau Center). This was built on the old Les Halles market site. It was very unusual. All the pipes, electric lines and building structures are exposed and the entire outside is like a scaffold with an escalator system ascending in a zigzag fashion to each level.

We went to the third level to see the Miro exhibit, and then walked around the modern paintings area. There was a library, office, exhibition hall, TV rooms and restaurant area all with the same exposed construction outside. We also saw a "Mime" like a beef eater, acting like a tin soldier as well as like a street performer eating lit cigarettes and 15 razor blades which he presumably chewed and then swallowed. There was also a toy exhibitor with little plastic wind up birds that flew around the room when they were wound up.

Then we walked around Rue de Sebastipol and finally found "Au Pied De Cochon" where we had lunch. It still looked the same with hûitres outside and delicious onion soup. I had the oysters and Al had fish. There were two young students sitting next to us, one from Tunis and one from France and we had a lovely conversation with them regarding the comparison of Paris France to New York and America. They were afraid that New York was too much like the movie "Taxi Driver" and then I overheard them discussing "truth" which the Tunisian said in French that "truth" is only whatever you believe, which is certainly an interesting concept.

After lunch we walked back to the Louvre and through the Tivoli Gardens and then on to the "Jeu De Paume" Museé which took quite a while to find, nevertheless it was fun walking through the gardens with the leaves crunching under foot and watching the nannies who were busy gossiping while their young children played near the swings. There were also old men playing Boule and the fountains sprayed amid the tall trees and there was a beautiful light that was flashing through the sky. (All very lovely sights!).

The Jeu De Paume has a wonderful collection of impressionistic paintings. There were many by Degas, Fantin Latour, Monet, Pissaro, Van Gogh, Berthe Morisot, Gauguin, etc. Among the most famous were Manet's "dejeuner in the grass", Van Gogh's "bedroom at Arles" and Renoir's "group at the café".

Regretfully we left the Museé at 5PM and Al and I walked back to the Crillion. It was a really long stretch although we stopped for some wonderful Italian grapes that came from Catania and were plump, sweet and delicious!

We also made a reservation for dinner at Andies which proved to be a big disappointment. First of all they were crowded with local diners and they shunted the foreigners (us) to a small section so we felt like second class citizens. Besides the food was not wonderful. I had eggplant puree, sliced veal with peas and carrots, and raspberries for dessert. Al had fish again (his favorite—not mine) which he said was tasty but not up to the standards of the majority of French restaurants.

After dinner we went to the George V where we met the Bachmans from Philadelphia (Joan and Jim). They were staying at our hotel and they told us that their son lives in Paris and has an adorable baby whom we saw the other day. We really do meet lovely people on our various trips which makes traveling so great.

Then we returned to Fouquets as we had promised to do and of course we were welcomed warmly by our waiter (Daniel) from the other night and believe it or not he refused to let us pay for our order and took the check himself. We could not believe that he really meant to do so. He told us about his family and particularly about his 10 year old daughter of whom he showed us a picture. We then exchanged addresses and we will send his little girl a nice present. We were really flabbergasted to think that Frenchmen would be so kind.

Of course I was now stuffed like a pig and was not sure I'd be able to go to bed although it was past midnight. Three more days of eating like this and I will most likely BURST!

Surprise! We just received a bottle of champagne from Harold and Jane Goldberg from Dallas. They really have been so considerate to us for so many years. After all we left Texas in 1945! Lucky us to have formed so many wonderful friendships.

Thursday, November 9th

We had our usual breakfast and there Al and I parted ways. I went to Celine's and he went to Air France and points west. Celine's did not have the bag I wanted so I walked to the Galeries Lafayette and bought a doll for Lizzie and a toy for Andy.

Then I simply shopped around until it was time to meet Al for lunch which we had at the "the Sherwood", recommended by the southerners we met at Raffatine and Honoré. We both had very good onion omelets after which we returned to the Rue De Rivoli where we stopped at Sagil and then meandered around buying odds and ends. We really were walking all over Paris which is the most marvelous place to do so.

Dinner was truly a treat. We went to the Doyen in the park. It was a most gorgeous restaurant. They had beige pleated fabric ceilings, interspaced with coral velvet beams which were placed in a diamond diagonal arrangement. There were Louis Fifteenth chairs, coral silk faille table cloths with beige lace over the cloths. There were yellow and coral roses in silver centerpieces, tall candles, and napkins with alençon lace corners. Everything was extremely lavish and the spacious foyer was like a beautiful huge living room. The dining room faced the gardens and there was a piano player and elegantly attired hovering waiters. Everything of course was extremely expensive but well worth it.

I had salad and fish hollandaise and Al had fish with lobster sauce. We also met some nice people from Houston, Texas at the next table. It was their first trip to Paris and they were ecstatic. Their names were Charlotte Abramson and something I don't remember (Kligman?). They too were in the jewelry business so there was a good deal of camaraderie with them and Al.

Again we did a bit of walking back to our hotel via the Champs Elyseé where we stopped to get Al some ice cream. I ordered some as well but they brought me the wrong flavor. Right now the air is a little nippier so I guess tomorrow will be quite cool.

Friday, November 10th—Kenny's Birthday

Today was really quite raw and actually it was the first day we felt any penetration of cold. Nevertheless we braved the frigid air and walked to the Rue Victor Hugo where I bought two lovely bags at Celine. That street is truly great for shopping, particularly the department store "Jones". There is also Prunière there and St Laurent Rive Gauche but since we really felt the chill down to our bones we stopped for some much needed hot chocolat and then taxied to the Louvre.

They now have the "Mona Lisa"—"La Jaconde" in a separate glass case, not like she was displayed years ago and the painting is still truly fantastic to behold. The eyes absolutely follow yours in every direction and so it was a great treat to be able to see her again. We also rediscovered the Venus De Milo who is still beautiful and of course the winged Victory of Samothrace enchanted us again.

After the wonders of the Louvre we went to "Pierre" for lunch which was Bobby Altman's recommendation but it looked very fancy (near drouant) so we elected to go to a creperie around the corner called "L'Opera Boûf "where we both had whole wheat crêpes with mushrooms, cheese, tomatoes, eggs, ham and spices. They were delicious accompanied by fizzy cider and then we shared an apple flambé crêpe as well.

On the way back to our hotel we stopped off to visit Lou Garlick who looked extremely well considering that he only left the hospital three days ago. He and Jewel had a beautiful suite with magnificent flowers in each room and after a nice visit with them we wandered into St. Laurent and I almost bought a pretty jacket but it was actually too small and they had no other sizes, so that was that.

After a nice rest period we realized it was again time to eat. We had a reservation at "le Lyonais" which had been recommended by Sophie Rothstein. It was a bit out of the way however the food was very good, although quite simple.

I had salad, coq au vin, and poire Helène avec chocolat. We had tea on the Champs Elyseé and then called Kenny in the U.S.A. Thankfully our connection was great which was quite amazing. We were sorry to miss his birthday but it was terrific speaking to him.

Saturday, November 11th

Armistice Day which was celebrated extensively in Paris began with a chill in the air like yesterday, however we still went out to the Champs Elyseé at 10 AM to watch the parade. I must say it was most impressive. We saw President Gistard D'Estaing reviewing the troops without a coat, plus many 4 star generals, and soldiers standing at attention all in array in their uniforms.

There were police on all the roof tops and many people lining the streets with their eyes riveted to the marchers. Everyone was bundled up because of the penetrating cold. There were also children on their father's shoulders, ladies in capes and boots, plus turtle neck sweaters were peeping out of all their jackets.

Each group of soldats had their own band which marched and played ahead of the soldats. We then saw the parachutists, the marines, the foot soldats, the air force, the naval group and finally the soldiers on horseback. This last group had their own band ahead of them and it was actually playing on horseback. Red, white, and blue lights shone in a floodlit beam and it was a most exciting sight. There were also thousands of young people out on the Champs Elyseé, many of them waiting on long lines to see the cinemas—just like in New York. I guess our cities are much the same when it comes to entertainment, even in the cold weather.

We had a lovely dinner at "Chez Joseph" which had a very art noveau type atmosphere. There were lace half curtains on the windows, art deco fixtures and chandeliers, little private booths outside the main portion of the dining room, and lovely green vines trellising all the way up the windows on the outside of the restaurant so that you could see them from the inside.

Our dinner consisted of tomato soup, rack of lamb with grilled tomatoes, sautéed leek potatoes dauphanais (scalloped with a biscuit cheese dough top and baked with a peppery sauce and was delish). Afterwards we had our usual tea on the Champs Elyseé and then we found our chestnut man on the avenue. The nuts were still positively great and hot hot hot!

Finally we walked through the Champs arcade which was a mad house of young people, many odd shops and a place that had disco records blasting loudly. There was also a MacDonald's which was crowded like the subway. Sadly this was our last night in Paris until who knows when!

Sunday, The Last Day

We awakened early and completed our packing. Happily the man from the belt store delivered my belts just as he promised which was so nice of him especially because it was a Sunday.

We then met the Bachmans and took the Metro with them to Montparnasse and Sacre Coeurr. The Metro was great fun. It was clean, speedy and attractive as well as being colorfully painted. Definitely not like American subways.

When we got to Sacre Coeur we walked up all the steps—what a climb! Whew! Then we had lunch outdoors, as by that time the weather became warm. We had marron crepes and tea and just about made it back to the hotel in time to pick up our luggage and taxi to the airport. Au Revoir Paris!

The flight home was great and thankfully we had the bulkhead seats again. The dinner on the plane was fine as well, which consisted of veal with artichoke bottoms, salmon, salad, crème caramel and tea

Finally! Home again and safe! Happy Days!!

New York To London
Thursday, May 14th 1979

I departed New York accompanied by Zelma and Buddy with much concern as it was my first European trip without AL. He was not able to go but it was a temple Israel trip so I presumed I would know several people other than the two of them.

The plane trip was mostly uneventful despite the fact that my seat neighbor twice spilled some juice and then some whisky all over me. Luckily the aisle seat allowed me to use some fast maneuvering in order to avoid getting completely drenched.

Also there was an amusing occurrence while I was on board when the stewardess made the following announcement. She said "the toilets are all filled so would everyone please return to their seats".

When we arrived in London there was great confusion and we were almost dragged bodily by an unruly guard who was pushing a group of baggage carts. However we finally found our way to the hotel by bus.

The hotel itself was unimpressive, the rooms were not ready and our tour group leader seemed generally incompetent. Nevertheless after a long wait we finally were ensconced in our rooms.

I then had lunch in the hotel dining room with Zelma and Buddy which was sort of a harrowing situation as Zelma really does come on rather strong. However we had a good lunch consisting of Old English style clam chowder, grilled steak with mushrooms and tomatoes, and orange flan pie for dessert.

We all ultimately went back to our rooms for brief naps as we intended going to the theatre that evening.

We saw "Conduct Unbecoming" that was a very good play about the English regiment in India and highlighted a quite deviate scandal which occurred therein. The performers were excellent and we had great seats as well. I must say the English theater is truly a wonderful experience.

Afterwards we went across the street to a little Chinese restaurant where we enjoyed our dinner immensely and then we returned to our hotel for a good night's sleep.

The next morning I found a message from Mr. Latham, the artist I met last year and from whom I had bought a painting. Hopefully I'll get to see him again as I really liked his artistic style and might possibly buy something else. AHA! I just got another call from him and we now have a date at Hyde Park on Sunday.

After having breakfast in the hotel's little coffee shop I went to Turnbull and Asser to shop for the "boys" back home (Kenny and Al). I bought a few nice sweaters and hope they will like my selection.

Portobello road was next where I went with the Gaines's. It was not as well stocked as it was on my last visit, but nevertheless it was an exciting and fun adventure.

Next I went back to the hotel for a pit stop and then continued on to the London Museum in Kensington Park right behind our hotel. Sylvia Gaines came with me. This Museum was originally Queen Victoria's childhood home and it housed her many mementos. Among the items were her wedding gown, her pony cart, various gowns belonging to her mother and also Princess Margaret's wedding gown which was quite unattractive (maybe that's why the marriage didn't last).

Victoria's gown was extremely small as she really was very tiny. Princess Charlotte's gowns were also gorgeous, as were many other lovely items belonging to all these ladies.

Then too there was an unusual painting of the original London Bridge which apparently was destroyed in 1842, and at that time it seemed to have a section that impeded the flow of water, and thus caused the Thames to freeze.

Back then they also used to have "frost fairs" on the River with very interesting booths, tents and skaters but it no longer freezes since the new bridge has been in place.

I met Zelma and Buddy for dinner at our hotel where we all had salad and roast beef served with an orange in Grand Marnier sauce with three strands of candied orange peel that was poured over the orange and was truly delicious. There was also a cherry on top of the entire thing.

After dinner we went to see a very good mystery play "Who Killed Santa Claus" with Honor Blackman. It had an odd twist at the end so we enjoyed the entire evening.

It became a late night's activity and therefore we didn't get to bed until midnight. (I couldn't stop yawning).

Sunday, May 17th

Then we had to get up early to go to Hyde Park to see the art show there, though it was not as good as the one last November, nevertheless I bought a nice sculpture from Mr. Latham.

It was extremely cold so I was happy to return to the hotel, but after warming up for a while I then decided to go to the National Gallery which was really fabulous. I saw Bellini's "The Doge", the "Van Eyke's", "The Marriage Couple" and many other old friends in the art world.

My next stop was the Ritz Hotel to which I walked the entire way and then I went to the Hyde Park exhibit next door.

I also bought some apples in the street that looked so good I could not resist them and finally went to Lottie Lubbock's for tea, where I enjoyed seeing her once again. There I had cod fish roe (tartan brand) with cucumber slices on top of a cracker. It was delicious and I certainly never had anything like it in America.

Returned to the hotel for a nap and had a late dinner with Zelma, Buddy and Steve (the tour leader). We had steak, salad with a lovely delicate whipped Roquefort dressing and some fruit for dessert. This thankfully was at the grill room of the hotel so we didn't have to venture forth and I was able to go to bed early.

Monday, May 18th

This morning I had breakfast with the Wechter's in the garden room which was a lovely place and besides the food was good, and I then went to Jaeger's with Sylvia Gaines where we both bought some nice clothes. After that we went to various other shops around Picadilly, Fortnum and Mason, W. Bill, etc.

We had a very good lunch in a little pancake house and then proceeded to the Royal Academy which was rather a disappointment. The artists were all unknown and not particularly exceptional.

When I returned to the hotel I found a message from my cousin John who lives near St. James Park. Zelma, Buddy and I are having lunch with him at Wheelers tomorrow, and we were really anxious to see him as it's been a few years.

I had dinner with the Gaines's and Wechters in the Grill and we all had that good steak again. Then we went to see "Hair". It really was a shocker, but extremely moving and exciting and also quite different. There were no holds barred and after a while the nudity etc. seemed commonplace. It was also sad and pathetic.

Bedtime finally and I really was tired!

Tuesday, May 19th

This morning I went to Goode's to check on my bill for Amy Becker's china and afterwards I proceeded to the tower of London which was a bit different from what I had expected.

The square where the actual beheading took place was much smaller than what I thought it would be but the tower area itself and the grounds as well appeared to be much larger. The place was most interesting although I found it to be quite touristy as well. The jewels of course were gorgeous.

After that I met Zelma and Buddy and we went to Wheelers where we had lunch with John. Everything was delicious especially my lobster au gratin and it was certainly great to see John. He loves living in London and has become quite English and European. I doubt if he will ever return to the states.

Then we went to the National Academy of Art where I saw a cartoon exhibit and also the latest painting of the Queen that

I did not like at all. It made her appear to be quite austere and plain.

My next stop was Foyle's book shop and finally I took the tube (subway) back to the hotel. The tube was really in the bowels of the earth but the seats were upholstered and had separate armrests. It was really a nice arrangement, and more comfortable than the New York subways.

Wednesday, May 20th (London to Amsterdam)

My breakfast was quite nice. I had eggs just the way I liked them (poached) then croissants with Elsenham's marmalade and tea. Then Buddy, Zelma and I took off for the airport. The flight was lovely but it arrived a half hour late.

They had a marvelous new system in the airport; it was a moving ramp that took you directly to your luggage without your having to walk. Then the ride to the hotel was really great. Every window in the attached houses that we passed was wide, spacious and sparkling and had beautiful voile and lace curtains. It was truly an incredible array and clean, clean clean!

The hotel was quite new and lovely, although we had to wait an hour before our rooms were ready. My room was beautiful and huge. It had an enormous bathroom also and every comfort seemed to be present.

We couldn't wait to visit the Rijksmuseum where we saw an eyeful of Rembrandt's galore, including "The Night Watch". The Jan Steens were marvelous and in general the museum was a fabulous treat.

This evening a dinner party was held in our honor and it was a pleasant surprise. We had shrimp cocktails, mushroom soup, chicken, Belgian string beans, salad and meringue pie with spun sugar on top. Divine and wunderbar! Then we walked around the hotel for a while and finally called it a night and went to bed.

Thursday, May 21st

This morning we went on a canal boat trip around the city that I thoroughly enjoyed although it was raining, however the boat was enclosed by glass so we were protected form the elements.

Again the windows in all the houses we passed were gleaming like mirrors. I wish I knew how they managed to keep them that way.

During the ride we also saw many little bridges and house boats and the entire trip was a quaint and charming sight.

Pretty soon we arrived at Anne Frank's house which I visited accompanied by Lenore Perlow with whom I went to grade school. The house was quite depressing, but important to see and remember. The steps were terribly steep which somehow added to the somber feeling and the realization of how desperate the times were during this girl's short life time were too terrible to dwell upon, and when we left the house it was difficult to return to more pleasurable activities and thoughts.

Rembrandt's house was where we ventured next and we were amazed at how wonderfully preserved the premises were. The walls had beautiful paneling and they were covered with his marvelous etchings. The equipment for producing them existed also.

I then walked to the Kalverstrasse, a considerable distance away but it was pleasant wandering amid the various shops. I bought a few lovely framed tiles and had lunch in a little place along the street. I had hot, hot, mushroom soup and terrific apple cake.

My next visit was to the Stavedelek museum to see the Van Gogh's which were absolutely something special and simply a marvelous experience. Also seeing some of the extreme modernists like Kowalski with all neon tubing and plexiglass, and someone named Bellmer or Bellmor (I don't quite remember his correct name) with his way out surrealistic drawings, made going to this museum a most unforgettable day.

I then had dinner with Zelma and Buddy, this included vichyssoise, which was very creamy and mild, then creamed "fruits de mer" in a puff pastry shaped like a fish. Dessert was fruit salad and everything was extremely good.

Since it became quite cold we just stayed at the hotel and spent time leisurely wandering into the many shops but did not make any purchases.

Friday, May 22nd

This morning I was up early for my nice breakfast of grapefruit, great pancakes and tea, and then got into the bus for our trip to Alkmaar, the cheese market. Our guide Joop was a fascinating person. He amazed us all with war stories about how his family hid some Jewish people, who later, (after the war) bought his family a house in gratitude and appreciation. He also explained the system of land reclamation in Holland that was complicated but ingenious.

En route we passed through Haarlem and saw the Droste factory plus some windmills which are necessary to maintain the water level.

Then at last we reached Alkmaar and that became a real fun experience. There were huge piles of cheese which were weighed and then put up for sale and purchased like in an auction. There were also basket makers, wooden shoe carvers, wooden plaque carvers, and calliopes playing jolly tunes. All this took place in a town square.

There were people in the area selling cheese samples, whole cheeses and apple puffs which were like hot doughnuts but much better. It was a most amusing sight to see, and I was also tempted to buy some of their wonderful copper items that I really loved but they were too big to carry. Oh well a person can't have everything.(But we can try!).

Finally we returned to the hotel for a short time and then went to Lassiter's studio. He was a very nice man and knew that both Kenny and I each owned one of his paintings. However I didn't see anything I absolutely had to have so I didn't make a purchase.

I did however buy a pretty Knirps umbrella at Bohner and wandered through the "Beehive" department store at the "Dam" monument. There apparently was a wonderful cookie shop called "Linde" near the "Dam" through an arcade but I couldn't find it so I just had a hot chocolate and some droste drops for lunch. While eating I glimpsed a very elegant wedding party which was surrounded by newspaper reporters and photographers so the couple must have been famous. All in all it was a pleasant afternoon.

Dinner time arrived and I dined alone at the hotel which I enjoyed for a change. I had vegetable soup, stuffed veal with spinach and rolled potato croquettes. My dessert was just a simple fruit salad after which I went to bed even though it was quite early. However I had a little sore throat so thought it was a good idea.

Saturday, May 23rd Amsterdam

Again I had a lovely breakfast, fried eggs and crisp bacon (which was almost bright red) and croissants with thick cherry jam and tea.

Afterwards I went downstairs to get on the bus as we were driving to a tulip bulb farm which was going to be our first stop. When we reached the farm we saw a gorgeous variety of tulips. The colors were most unusual and there were also many hybrid types, certainly not at all like what was available in America. To say the least it was a tremendously picturesque spot.

Then we drove on to Schevenger the Beach Resort, which was a charming spot that had extremely wide flat reefs and there were loads of people walking on them. The beach itself was a fairly flat area that faced the water which flowed into the North Sea. A pavilion similar to one in Atlantic City was at the end of a pier.

Many little night clubs and motels etc were also in this little town which was very quaint. We continued on to Maduradam for lunch which we had near an absolutely, marvelously, ingenious, reconstruction of a miniature "Amsterdam and Hague" down to the last detail. It consisted of a little airport, ships, barges, public buildings, water falls and bonsai trees. It was a complete replica of the towns and was a truly worthwhile sight.

We also passed the "real Hague" which was a fairly commercial layout so we simply rode by the most noteworthy institutions.

After that we went to Rotterdam, a amazing place that was almost completely destroyed during the Second World War and therefore had to be reconstructed in the major portions of the city. Here were a lot of brightly colored plastic and technical displays attributed to the fairs and commercial shows that are held there, and a cute little tramway circled the main streets. All in all this was quite a busy day, but wearying and pleasant. Thank heavens the weather was exceptionally nice.

After we returned to the hotel we all had a very nice dinner in the Diamond grill which was a lovely room where they generally held large affairs so it was suitable for dancing as well. My dinner was consommé, poached salmon with mushrooms, a great salad and a ginger ice cream sundae.

Ho Hum, I'm exhausted and we leave here in the morning.

Sunday, May 24th—Amsterdam to Copenhagen

I arose early and had a nice breakfast consisting of pancakes etc. Then I had to gather my luggage together which was a real chore and had to pay $7.00 overweight for it at the airport. Then I had to drag the bags to the plane for boarding. Most of the group bought watches etc in the free port but I just purchased some liquor for Al.

Lunch on the plane was really good and consisted of hot rolls, delicious ham, marvelous potato salad and little string beans, macaroni and cheese, plus apple juice and tea.

There was nothing particularly eventful on the flight except for my having to drag my bags again to the bus. I felt like singing "Tote That Barge—Lift That Bale".

Nevertheless when we got to the hotel excitement prevailed! When we looked at the rooms we all almost fainted! The place was a real flea bag. The rooms were tiny and most of the bathrooms did not have either a tub or a shower, just a drain in the floor. Unbelievable! Actually I was one of the lucky ones as I had a half tub.

However on the 6th floor the rooms were much nicer but the entire group was up in arms—Mutiny! There was a general meeting and some people were all set to go home immediately.

I however called Zelma's friend Pearl who was staying at the Kong Frederick Hotel and she was able to get rooms for me and Zelma and Buddy. So we left the "dreadful Dan" and found ourselves at a most wonderful old world hotel with beautiful rooms, and modern bath accommodations. The rooms had lovely brass and wood pieces and in general we all felt much better. In addition to the great hotel itself, they had the cutest little doorman about 4 foot high and he was an adorable and kind addition to our lovely surroundings.

We did not know what our arrangements would be as far as meals were concerned but hoped to find out at the dinner for us that evening at the Dan Hotel.

Miraculously our dinner was wonderful (I guess to make up for the discomfiture of the rooms, but of course that no longer concerned us). At any rate we had a tiny Danish shrimp cocktail in Russian dressing, very good steak, green beans, potatoes, salad and an ice cream cake. Then they sent up a series of fireworks which was most spectacular.

Most of the group was still unhappy but we of course were thrilled with our rooms in the Kong Frederick.

Monday, May 25th—Copenhagen

We all had a lovely breakfast, tasty Danish, rolls and tea in the nice breakfast room downstairs. My room was charming and the walls were all paneled, and as I mentioned before there was lots of brass, but also etched glass. It was an unusual and very attractive room and in one of the nicest hotels in Europe so far.

Then I went down to the canal boat landing for our boat tour. This was particularly interesting as we stopped and took pictures of the "Little Mermaid" at the water's edge. She was smaller than I had imagined, but was adorable.

We also stopped at the King's library and garden and the sculpture presented by the Jews to the Danes for rescuing services during the War were extremely poignant to see.

After that we visited the Jewish Street with Ann Cohen's butcher shop and many other points of interest including the royal yacht and a hydrofoil that goes directly to Sweden. Our lunch was at the Kong Frederick where I had a Monte Cristo sandwich and tea.

Pearl and I then walked through the strôget(the shopping street) which was loads of fun as there were no cars allowed so it was easy to just amble along.

We also went to the Royal Copenhagen store next, where I bought a beautiful blue and white tea set and avidly admired all the gorgeous china and porcelain. They even demonstrated the decorating of the china while I was there.

I luckily ate some good pastry that I purchased in the street and also bought apples and cookies for our trip tomorrow.

Then back at the hotel I took a tub bath which I hadn't had in a long time but it was a welcome change, although I really prefer a shower.

Dick Sondheim then came by and paid me $100 Kroner for my hotel room at the Dan which was quite nice of him as I wasn't going to use it anyway.

Dinner was next with Zelma, Pearl and Buddy at the "Au Coq D'or", a charming little place with delicious food, and I had very good asparagus soup, baked chicken with mushrooms, tomato and bacon plus fried paisley salad and tea. No dessert.

Zelma was upset because the restaurant had no tablecloths so we had to walk out at first, finally though she gave in and we returned. She is really very nervous (or spoiled?).

Tuesday, May 26th—Copenhagen

I had my usual breakfast downstairs and then walked to the Royal Hotel to meet the tour bus. Our first stop this time was Fredericksborg Castle which was a magnificent structure filled to the brim with gorgeous furnishings, including wonderful ceramics, etc.

The chapel was marvelous too with beautiful plaques on the wall for the "order of the elephant", some of which had been presented to Churchill, Eisenhower, etal. One unusual painting was much like a venetian blind in a vertical alignment with a King painted on one end and a Queen on the other, also it was pleated, strange but attractive.

We then passed by the Deer Park where the King hunts and also through some nice little villages along the way.

Our final stop was at Elsinore's Kronberg Castle where the story of Hamlet originated. This one was not as magnificent as the other castle, but was interesting and boasted of the largest reception Hall in Europe. It was quite spare, nevertheless it was attractive.

We also ate some little snacks on the bus and returned to the Hotel until our afternoon outing.

Den Permanente was the P.M. destination where it was fun to admire the modern and unusual items, however it started to rain heavily so we taxied to illiums' small store by mistake, and since we only had a short time left to shop, we expected to return to the large illiums store tomorrow.

We had made a reservation at Krogs for dinner with Pearl and we arrived there at 7:30 in the rain and bumped into Sylvia Gaines so we all ordered the same thing, fish "tout Paris". This was excellent and lovely to behold. It was a large hot platter with Duchess potatoes all around and in between it was sectioned off to house various items of food, tiny peas, mushrooms, little shrimp, asparagus, fried plaice (flounder), filet of sole in a lobster sauce, little tomatoes and lemon slices for a garnish, and Hollandaise sauce on the side. It was all delicious, and then we had beer and tea.

Unfortunately Pearl had an awful coughing fit on the way out of the restaurant so we had to remain there for a while.

Then after we returned to the hotel, I went to her room with her to be sure she was okay and while there I went to the bathroom. However when I came out I didn't see her and couldn't imagine how she could have disappeared as it was such a small room. Finally after I closed the bathroom door which opened out, there she was behind the door so we both got hysterical laughing.

Since she obviously was alright we decided to go to Tivoli which was really something to behold.

It appeared to have a million colored lights, red, blue, green and yellow on a small lake that was all lit up. There were also many illuminated restaurants, an outdoor concert hall, and an outdoor ballet which we watched.

It was really an unusual experience. Then we went to a place for hot chocolate and a mocha éclair, both of which were delicious. However this place seemed like an old world Viennese restaurant, as it had violins playing and at any moment I expected Hitler to pop out, a most uncomfortable feeling. At any rate we enjoyed ourselves and had a few laughs.

On the way back to the Kong Frederick we met Zelma and Buddy, who apparently had eaten dinner at the hotel and had a good time. Thank heavens Zelma enjoyed herself. Bed Time now—Snore—Snore!

Wednesday, May 28th

I had breakfast downstairs as usual and fantastically it was a glorious day weather wise and especially after yesterday's rainfall, it was most welcome so I started to walk on Strôget Street where I bought a lovely pantsuit, and saw many other things suitable for young people. It is really a young city.

Finally I got to illiums (the large one) which was a sensational place with fabulous items. I saw a lovely group of blue and white china from Sweden and many other exciting and unusual things but I thought I had made enough purchases on this trip so had to forego any more.

I then met Zelma and Buddy at Oscar Davidson's for lunch where they had smorgasbord and It was divine. They had all manner of delicious food stuffs including very good ice cold beer, so I am now fat, fatter and fattest.

Since we were going to the ballet tonight I had to return to the hotel to organize my packing as we only have one more day in Copenhagen.

When I got to the Ballet Theatre with Pearl she started coughing terribly again and could not stop therefore she decided to return to the hotel.

Luckily I was able to sell her ticket to a nice Danish lady and I spent a delightful evening sitting next to her. As an added fillip, the King and Queen were in the royal box. It was truly exciting. The Queen was charming in appearance and waved to everyone. She is Ingrid of Sweden, mother of Anne Marie of Greece.

The lady next to me, (Mrs. Lingner) told me that she and the Queen go to the same hairdresser on Tuesdays and the Queen sits next to her. Also Mrs. Lingner's husband is studying to be an archeologist even though he owns a farm in the countryside. They have 3 children and she has been to America where she bought some beautiful jewelry at Marchals.

My vacation time is just about over and it was most enjoyable. It is too bad that Al couldn't have been with me.

Farewell

Mona Lisa

PARIS
Friday, October 4th—Saturday, October 5th, 1979

There is nothing as wonderful as another trip to our favorite city, Paris. This time we were traveling with the Lawrence golf club accompanied by the Cedars and Goodmans. TWA was the airline of choice and all of us were excited to finally be taking off.

Louise and Larry Miller were also on the same flight but they intended driving through the wine country. Louise told us that she is currently in charge of the Morgan Library art exhibits, which sounded fascinating, and of course she is certainly worthy of that position as her talent in the art field is well known.

Unfortunately there was a slight mix up on the flight so we had to change our seating arrangements, and besides that the dinner that was served was not good. There was no tea available, and nothing that took place was as nice as Air France was last year. Therefore we did not think we were off to a successful start vacation wise.

However when we arrived at the Lotti hotel, wonder of wonders, things improved. The bedroom was large, square and most attractive and the bathroom was huge and modern so all in all it suddenly seemed to be a nice beginning to our vacation after all.

Of course we were quite weary after the flight, so first we napped and then we went to Stella Artois (a bistro nearby) where I had soup, chestnuts and a patisserie custard tart and Al had soup as well, plus an apple tart.

Then we walked about for a while and after that we returned to the hotel to change for dinner at Le Soufflé.

There we were given a private room with our group, and the food was not too bad. We had artichoke bottoms with mushrooms in a mayonnaise sauce on top (too rich by far). Then came chicken with tarragon and potatoes. The potatoes they served were too doughy, although the hot chocolat soufflé was quite good, but not chocolaty enough. After dinner we sat around chatting with the group but finally gave into our wearied state and went to bed completely affected with first day exhaustion.

Saturday, October 5th

We had a wonderful night's sleep and were thoroughly refreshed and ready to enjoy what appeared to be a beautiful day. When we looked out our windows the Paris roof tops looked like little grey teeth in the sky, which was quite weird.

Our Petit Dejeuner which arrived promptly, was the usual croissants and jam plus some wonderful bread and tea, after which we showered, dressed and went downstairs for a nice walk.

Then we joined our group for a bus tour that turned out to be a great deal of fun as we went to places we'd never seen previously i.e. the Place Des Vosges (Victor Hugo's birthplace) and also Madam De Sevigney's home, which was very charming on an old square in a lovely area with restored homes that had recently been converted to apartment houses.

Afterwards we left the bus and took the Cedars and Goodmans to Au Pied De Cochon for lunch and all of us had their wonderful onion soup and niçoise salad which was still as good as it always had been.

Then we walked back to Rue St Honoré and did some shopping. After all "girls will be girls". So first we went to Alice Landais and bought some lovely chiffon scarves upon which we were able to have our names embroidered if we so desired. Then we walked into the Charles Jourdan shop where we all bought very exciting shoes. Mine were a combination of black and purple. Unexpectedly we met Nadia Stark there and after chatting with her for a while we continued on to "Catherine" for perfume and face creams.

Wearily we had to return to our hotel for a rest period before dinner which was slated for "Rostang". This restaurant was owned by the people from "La Bonne Auberge" in Antibes and had an interesting presentation of food. There were little flakey sticks with black pepper, tiny radishes, tomatoes and shrimp, then salade with thin string beans and artichokes. We were then served fish (lotti) pieces with zucchini and more tomatoes and finally tea with wonderful blown up cookies with slivered nuts, madelaines, glazed grapes, strawberries and kumquats. Everything was really exceptional.

Another couple joined us (Si and Roz Deutch), who knew my cousin Ruth Kantor which made our evening sort of a Jewish geography situation.

Then we returned to the Goodman's suite for a short time and finally called it a day and went to bed.

Sunday, October 7th

We had an early petit dejeuner and then went to the lobby to meet Nadia. Larry was already waiting for her and when Phyllis finally arrived we went to the flea market which was exactly how I thought it would be. It was much like Portobello Road.

Nadia bought several rugs at "Sergio" while I mosied about and saw an interesting writing box with two hidden drawers. I really coveted it but the salesman said someone else had already put a deposit on it—too bad.

We all went to the Plaza Athenée for lunch at the Relais. The hotel was still as beautiful as we saw it on our first trip to Paris and the lunch was also extremely tasty. I had eggs on spinach, a lovely tomato salad and an apricot tart.

Nadia was most pleasant and the restaurant was buzzing with smartly dressed people but soon Trudy Gleckel arrived from London and joined us (She really looked liked a Zombie after her plane ride).

We then all proceeded to the Swiss Village where Nadia looked at several more rugs but did not buy any.

Afterwards we all went to L'Isle St. Louis which was a charming place somewhat like Greenwich Village. There were lovely boutiques near the "Alexandre Pont" and we all wandered about until a taxi arrived and AL and I and the Cedars returned to our hotel. Nadia and Trudy of course kept on going no doubt to make more purchases somewhere.

Dinner this time was at Chez Michel with the Goodmans and Cedars and the food was delicious. We had cheese popovers, little olives, and mushrooms first, and then salad, rack of lamb with French fries, and raspberry feuilleté was our wonderful dessert.

Our taxi was still waiting for us so we went to the Crillion for a while and then walked leisurely back to our hotel where the whole Lawrence group were sitting around and chatting about their adventures during that day.

By this time we were both hopeful that we'd be able to spend the next day alone so we could do as we wished. It would certainly be preferable to make our gift purchases by ourselves.

Monday, October 8th

We arose early and had our usual petit dejeuner after which Nadia called and said she would not join us for dinner as Trudy whom we did not invite, might have felt slighted.

Then we went to Laurentious for ties and also to a children's shirt factory next door. The owner was Jewish and said he recognized Al's name as originating from Spain. Who knows we may have Spanish relatives.

Afterwards we walked back to the Opera Bouffe to our little creperie from last year next to Pierre's and Café Drouant, and then to Victor Hugo to see Nancy's boutique. However we discovered that the place was actually their home and it was a positively gorgeous apartment. The door was opened by a black servant garbed in a purple jelaba. The foyer had a black grand piano in one corner and the carpeting was dark blue that had an oriental rug on top. Also there was a coramandel screen in another corner with a Lucite pedestal topped by an attractive sculpture in front of the screen. There was a large painting on another wall and we were also able to glimpse into the dining room which had an exceptionally lovely lacquered dining table. On the other side of the foyer was a huge living room but all we noticed there was a magnificent Chinese Chest. The whole room was terrific but we couldn't be too obvious about looking around.

Al returned to our hotel and I proceeded to Rodier where I bought a pretty knit dress and a sweater. I also purchased two bags at Celine but had to leave them there as they would not accept a Master Charge card so I have to return tomorrow with my American Express card.

I then took a bus to Foubourg St. Honoré (down Ave Friedland) and sauntered around there before returning to the hotel where I finally succumbed to the rigors of shopping and rested until dinner.

Dinner was at LeDoyen which was still a gorgeous restaurant in the park and we had fish with hollandaise sauce, salad and raspberries with cream. Ho Hum again—This was really a weary day. Good Night!

Tuesday, October 9th

Again we arose early to witness a gloomy grey morning from the windows, although the sun was expected to pop out any minute.

I met Phyllis downstairs and we both went to the Galerie Lafayette to shop for our grandchildren. They didn't have much of a selection but I did manage to buy a few things for Lizzie and Andy.

In the afternoon Al and I went to the left bank by bus to Maud Frizon which was a big disappointment. The selection was limited, not at all like New York, however I did return to Celine for my bags and got one for Nancy as well. Then we went by bus again to Rue De Madelaine and the weather became miraculously wonderful, balmy, sunny and ideal for American tourists.

We had dinner at L'Orangerie, which was charming although rather narrow. It had a beamed ceiling and had lovely wainscoating. There was also an enormous 5 foot bouquet of flowers on the bar.

Surprisingly we were the first arrivals but soon the place was jammed with beautiful women and handsome men in gorgeous clothes. The ladies wore fabulous jewelry. One lady was wearing what appeared to be a 22 ct diamond ring, another one had a white, grey and black pearl necklace, and they all had exquisite hairdo's, chignons or loose arrangements. They wore perfect make up and wore either red satin or blue satin shirts with black skirts. Très chic!

The dinner was price prixe, wine, bacon and poached eggs, thin sliced veal with mustard sauce, mashed turnips and raspberries with crème fraiche and rolled cookies were served from a tin box. The atmosphere was lovely and the food was good, although the personnel were not too pleasant. Maybe they didn't want a tourist clientele. We went to bed early as we leave tomorrow.

Wednesday, October 10th—Amsterdam

We had to be up early so we decided to walk outside for a while to say goodbye to beautiful Paris and of course we both hope to return here again someday.

We got to the airport and had a nice flight to Amsterdam. I sat next to a woman on the plane who was a Pharmacist and who works in the medical department of Chemalex which is part of Phillips Drugs. She told us she had a summer home on the water in Carnac (she's French) that had big oak trees that grow inside the house and she said they call the house "something special".

Finally we arrived at the hotel and thankfully we were in a lovely room. There were gold fixtures in the bathroom, the room had Murphy beds and a lovely terrace. The weather was gorgeous and all's right with our world.

Believe it or not we had a little tea party in our room with the Cedars and then went for a canal ride.

I recalled several things from having been here before, particularly the hooks on the various buildings we passed that are used for hoisting furniture as the steps in the buildings are too narrow to accommodate large pieces, and also #7 the smallest house on the water which is just the width of a window in the "gentlemen's canal".

We then returned to the hotel for a nap and dinner in the downstairs dining room, which was a far cry from Paris. We had a fairly nice salad from a salad bar, wafer thin cukes, cabbage, beets, land cress, olives and tomatoes, etc. but unfortunately the soup was cold so we sent it back to the kitchen (I hoped they didn't spit in it!).

Then we had lamb with carrots and flageletts which I gave to Al. Sadly it was not a good dinner. After dinner we went to the red light district and saw the young girls in the window facing the street, which was an incredible sight. I guess I'm really a prude, but it was tawdry and sad. They also had many sex shops with all kinds of devices for sexual performances. It was an amazing place really like another world. Then too they also had porno movies, and hardcore shops which they advertised as "Fucky Fucky" shows and I couldn't help feeling sorry for all these young girls. What a horrid way to make a living.

We then went to an outdoor gelati place and had an ice cream cone and so to bed. It was really too bad that we came here after Paris because it was impossible to compare the two cities.

October 11th, Thursday

Al and I both awakened about 5:30 AM because of a loud drilling clatter in the street below us and since it kept up until

6:30 AM we lost our sleep until that time. Afterwards we slept until 8:30 AM and had to rush like mad to catch the bus at 9:30 AM for our daily tour.

We just had time for a scant breakfast, a raisin roll, tea and some Kimmel cheese which we were able to have in the lovely breakfast room downstairs. This room was surrounded by beautiful palms and was airy and pleasant.

The bus then took us to the Jewish temple which was beautiful although it had no electricity just candles on every pew. The brass chandeliers were quite attractive as well, and all the seating was arranged in 3 tiers with seats that lifted up so that prayer books could be put inside. A clever idea indeed.

The next stop was the Rijksmuseum where we saw Rembrandt's "Night Watch" which was now displayed behind a protective sheet of glass as it had been vandalized and slashed last year.

A diamond factory was also on the agenda which of course was not of particular interest to us as we have been to so many of them in the states.

At last lunch time arrived but that was most unsatisfactory. It was just soup and grapefruit sections in wine and served by an extremely rude waiter.

However, we were able to compensate for that unsatisfactory situation by buying lovely pastry (chocolate éclairs with schlag) at a little place called the Beehive.

Anne Frank's house was next on the list and it appeared to be smaller than I remembered from the last time I saw it, but it still gave me an eerie feeling. It is really hard to believe what a terrible time that was for Jewish people and sadly that it might happen again.

We finally went to the Schartze Shweep for dinner after roaming around to four different restaurants and thankfully this one was delicious. We had a marvelous niçoise salad, bread with garlic butter and veal steak with fried onions which was really great and it was served with carrots, bean pods and potatoes. (I can't believe I am eating all this food).

Then we took a trolley car back to Dam Square from the restaurant and passed through a lively area with lots of young people, restaurants, clubs and movies. The buses that we saw were very quaint. They were narrow, pointed in the front, and moved quickly. Strangely on our trolley car they never collected the fare. (Maybe they were being nice to tourists).

Afterward we stopped for gelati from a cute little stand and then sat in our hotel lobby with the Liebmans from Margaret Avenue in Lawrence, for a while. Time for bed suddenly arrived so good night!

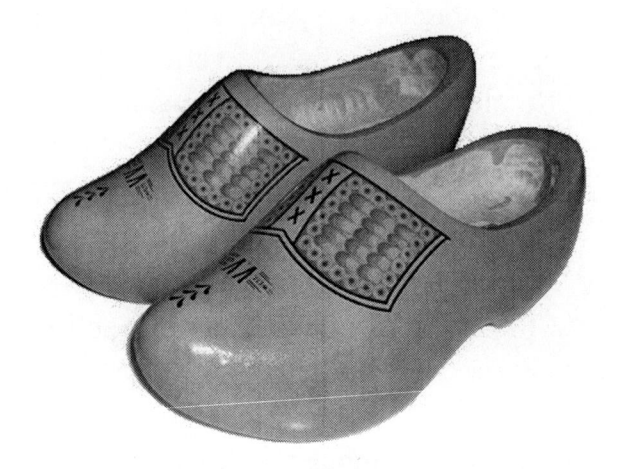

Friday, October 12th

Too Bad! We woke up to one of the first rainstorms we ever had on a European vacation, so we had a leisurely breakfast of cheese, sesame crisp and tea and finally went downstairs to take our tour bus to a cheese farm.

We passed farms, dykes and cows etc on the way and ultimately stopped at an interesting place where we saw a funny fellow with a hilarious accent demonstrating the making of Gouda cheese. He could easily have been a stand up comedian and of course we all bought cheese and ceramic plates. Our bus then took us to Vollendam where we saw many fishing boats and souvenir shops and while there our guide Vera ate a whole herring in one gulp—Wow! The entire village was most appealing and of course we all bought little odds and ends just like most tourists do.

Marken was our next stop, which was the same kind of village but a tad smaller than Vollendam. While there we saw a man carving wooden shoes and they served us a delicious hot chocolate while we watched him.

So far this bus trip was lots of fun, except that Al developed a chill and a stomach ache. So we ultimately went back to our hotel room where we had a picnic lunch with the Cedars. Luckily we had some food left over from two breakfasts, cheese, etc.

Then Phyllis and I took the #16 bus to the New Van Gogh Museum where it was a pleasure to see all the wonderful paintings I had seen on my previous trip to Amsterdam, particularly the 'potato eaters" and Vincent's "room at Arles".

We then took a fast walk down Kalvestraet for about 10 minutes, ate some cookies and then returned to our hotel.

Al was still not in good shape so we decided to have an early dinner at the Oyster Bar with the Cedars and Clara and Larry Rosenthal who had just arrived in Amsterdam from Egypt. They told us that they had a great time and I hope maybe someday Al and I will go there. There are so many places we would love to see in this remarkable world if only there was time to see it all.

At the Oyster Bar we had some good vegetable soup, salad, fish with tiny shrimps, crab meat and mushroom sauce all over the fish (sole). We also drank beer as well.

We then returned to the hotel by trolley car and this time we had to pay our fare. The other three times we rode we did not pay so I presumed the driver now considered us to be natives. Although we since found out that payment is on the honor system, where you can ride free for an hour after your ticket is stamped, which is a good system, but of course since we did not know about it, we simply did not pay on our other trips, however I don't think we will receive a jail sentence for our free trips.

Bed time arrived and we packed our belongings in order to be ready to leave in the morning for London.

We arrived at the Amsterdam airport and bought some cheese for Kenny. I could also have bought a beautiful purple belt for $14. But I didn't have enough guilders left—too bad—next time maybe.

Saturday, October 13th—London

The flight was fine but the Strand Palace in London was anything but. We all had to leave the hotel as our rooms were not ready so we walked to Fortnum and Mason's for lunch. After eating a great chicken pie and a raspberry soda we returned to the hotel only to find that our room was terrible. It was completely inadequate. We tried to change to no avail tonight but they promised us much better accommodations tomorrow. Unfortunately we had to sleep there for one night.

The Cedars were distraught, as well as some of the other members of our group, although some people were given lovely rooms.

We enjoyed a lovely cocktail hour at the Berkley with the Goodmans as they were able to get a lovely room there.

Then we all proceeded to Wheelers for dinner. I had a crab cocktail, good bread and Dover Sole Bonne Femme. It had mushrooms and herbs and was really delicious.

Afterwards we walked around Regent Street past Acquascutum etc, and ultimately arrived at The Savoy for a drink. That was seedy too, however we met a Jewish man (he may have been an actor), in the lobby who kiddingly offered us his suite. We were sorely tempted to accept it but unfortunately we had to return to our dreadful room for just that night.

Sunday, October 14th

We both awakened with headaches as the room was stifling and at 6 AM we went down to breakfast where thank heavens the food was good even though it was just croissants, jelly and juice.

Then we got on a bus to ride around the city which was pleasant indeed and after that we went to the Waldorf Hotel to see if they had any empty rooms. But even though the hotel was charming, they had no vacancies. However we finally got better rooms in our hotel and it was now quite comfortable. The Cedar's new room was not as nice as ours and they were very upset and still tried to move elsewhere.

We then went to a pancake house for lunch and afterwards proceeded to the Speakers Corner which was always entertaining, so Al and Larry stayed there to listen to the speeches while Phyllis and I walked along the Hyde Park fence and bought a few odds and ends; she got shoe buckles and I bought a nice drawing.

Finally we went back to the hotel to rest and hopefully to find a good restaurant for dinner.

Luckily we wound up at the White Elephant Club on the River by using Arnold Neustadter's name which worked. The place was absolutely lovely with beautiful paintings for sale around the walls. There was also a wonderful view of the river and the walls were all sepia colored with white moldings. We had drinks at the bar accompanied by nice little tidbits, followed by a terrific dinner.

I had an artichoke, a veal chop with mushrooms and tomatoes, onions and herbs plus little potatoes. There was also linguini Bolognaise which was delicious, and tea. They served us petit fours, glazed kumquats and strawberries etc, plus the waitress came around with a fabulous dessert wagon with oranges, St. Honoré cake, mousse and several other enticing items.

We met three lovely people there from San Francisco. Two were lawyers and one used to be married to the owner of the Dollar Line. They had just taken an apartment in London for the winter which seemed to be a good idea. Finally it was bed time after a mostly harrowing day.

Monday, October 15th

We had a nice breakfast and then taxied to Jaegers where we bought 2 skirts for me plus a shirt and scarf, then sweaters for Al and Kenny and a blouse for Nancy. The clothes were lovely and we could have bought more if we had more time.

New Bond Street came next where it was fun to mosey about. Then we went to W. Bill and finally to Fortnum and Mason for sodas. I had a great raspberry soda there and then we returned to our hotel where we just had a little light snack (soup and dessert) as we were going to an early show in the evening.

Al saw "whose life is it anyway" and I saw "Crusifer in Blood" which had wonderful sound and stage effects, with boats on the stage and real fog coming out into the audience, lightening and thunder prevailed and all in all it was very contrived but the show itself was not terrific!

Afterwards we went to the Savoy Hotel for hot chocolate with the Cedars. We were all extremely tired so bedtime was next. Goodnight!

Tuesday, October 16th

We slept a little late this AM and then had breakfast in the hotel's carving room as it was too late to have it in the breakfast lounge.

Then we taxied to "Browns" on South Molton. This was Shirley Becker's favorite shop. The street itself is a walking street with beautiful shops, somewhat like Worth Avenue in Palm Beach.

Everything in Brown's was lovely and we actually spoke to the proprietor about Nancy's Bags. They were quite interested in buying some of them. I'm supposed to send them pictures of them when I get home. They carry Maud Frizon shoes and of course many other well known brands of items from many countries.

Our next stop was Grey's Antique Market but we didn't make any purchases there. However I did buy a pretty sweater at Marks and Spencer, and then walked to the Churchill Hotel, which I believe is on Oxford Street and where we met Lottie Lubbock for lunch. She looked wonderful, and we had a drink plus a not exactly marvelous lunch. It consisted of a Spanish omelet that had no tomatoes and was devoid of flavor, oh well at least I would not gain weight from eating it so that was comforting.

Renie Harrison was supposed to join us but wasn't feeling well. However we had a great time with Lottie who told us that Jules is now an art lecturer at a University and is writing a book on art. He also is a very good friend of Prince Charles. She also mentioned that her son Richard is presently a well known television writer in Toronto. It was nice to hear that her family seems to be doing well.

Chester Barrie was next on our list but Al could not find any suits he liked so I left him to continue his shopping elsewhere and I went to Jaegers myself and bought a camel hair skirt, a really pretty one and then I went to Fortnum and Mason for their marmalade which I love.

Being exhausted I returned to the Hotel to find that Renie Harrison had called. She was so sorry not to have seen us and was hoping we would be able to get together in a few days.

Also apparently her granddaughter Rosalie (?) Burris was moving to New York. She is 24 and a journalist and Renie wondered if Kenny would call her. Maybe he will.

After resting a while we dressed and went to Cecconi's for dinner. This was a truly beautiful and excellent restaurant recommended to us by Dorothy Neustadter who certainly has great taste. It is on New Bond Street opposite Ferragamo and next to Waterford Crystal, a truly chic place with bone fabric walls, bone braid trim, bone Chippendale chairs and brass sconces with lovely shades on the bulbs.

Our dinner was grissini, risotto with vegetables (The Cedars had this) green noodles, ham, cheese and cream. (Al and I had this), then we all had veal with lemon, zucchini and a slice of tiny round eggplant which was stuffed. Dessert was a raspberry whipped cream feuillité tart. Everything was really delicious,(divine is probably a better word.)

The restaurant was filled with very chic people. One girl was wearing a hand painted flowered gold llamé jacket, another one was wearing a black skirt and an antique cream colored satin shirt with a Bertha lace collar on top. There were many other outstanding appearing people, all of whom seemed to be from London. Somehow it was apparent that they were not from America.

After this sumptuous feast we returned to the hotel to organize our packing as tomorrow we go to Broadway and possibly Blenheim. It will be a big travel day as we expect to be gone the entire time and will have to get up early in the morning.

Wednesday October 17th

We left the hotel at 8 Am via a little bus, en route to Bladen, to see Winston Churchill's tomb in a quiet little village cemetery. Then we continued on to Broadway which is a well known country town in the Cotswold, where there is a charming inn and where we thought it would be wonderful to stay for a few days if we had time. It is called the "Lygon Arms". The place is very old and typically English.

We had lunch at a darling little pink and green tea room. First we had celery soup, then a "pastie" pie filled with meat, and lastly we had a watercress and egg sandwich, and lemon meringue pie with whipped cream, all of which was delicious. I do believe that all of us will have gained many pounds on this trip which may necessitate purchasing an entirely extra sized wardrobe.

After that we continued on to Anne Hathaway's cottage in Stratford on Avon. It had a thatched roof and old gardens with original plantings. The inside of the house had dark beams and all the old original furnishings. We also passed Shakespeare's' graveyard and the town itself was most charming.

Then we continued on to Blenheim Palace, which was The Duke of Marlboro's home. (Consuelo Vanderbilt was married to one of the Dukes, Gloria's Aunt I believe). The home was gorgeous. There were wonderful paintings by Sargent and Romney, and also Winston Churchill was born there in a beautiful brass bed (very short) in a rose strewn wallpapered room. In the dining room there was lovely white (blanc de chine) china and an unusual blue china. The Duke was in residence at that time so we could not see his quarters.

The library was magnificent, sort of a pale peachy tan with white moldings and a sky blue ceiling, and they had blue sofas all around with coral, peach, lime green and olive green pillows. Everything there was truly unforgettable and it simply exuded great wealth.

Once again we returned to London and went to Harrods for candy and then to Sloane's café for a hamburger and beer. We were now ready to pack up for our trip home tomorrow. This was, as usual a lovely vacation and it is finally time to face reality.

      Goodbye London—Hello America!

Morocco and Monte Carlo
Saturday, October 2nd 1982

Another trip—This time we left for Casablanca on Air Maroc, with the Goodmans, Sunas and Cedars. It was with the Lawrence Golf Club group tour.

We had an unsatisfactory dinner on the plane. Awful chicken, a gluey dessert and a mediocre salad.

However we arrived safely after having seen a glorious sunrise. It was all red and we also saw a beautiful soft cloud formation over the water that looked like white fluff. What can be better than nature at its best?

We went directly into a new plane at Casablanca, and then continued by bus to the hotel Mamounia in Marrekesh. This was a beautiful red clay hotel behind red clay walls with horses completely covered with flies guarding the entranceway, and miraculously they never moved. (the horses not the flies).

There were lovely flowers and trees (orange and lime trees) Bougainvillea, cypress, palm trees, roses, verbena and morning glorys all around the hotel. In addition there was a glorious pool area with a large gazebo where lunch was served, and also a huge fountain in the water that sprayed continually, and in the lobby there were large crystal fixtures much like the ones in the Doral lobby.

Apparently there were some very nice people on this trip. Dr. Harold Cook and his wife Honey who were good friends of Ruth Roman and Si and Roz Deutch from our last trip. She was the lady who kept us supplied with candy.

Unfortunately we had a bad lunch in the grill if you can figure out how an omelet can be bad. However the service was also terrible so that made it a double whammy.

Then we had our dinner in the hotel dining room which was a lovely place but the food was just as bad as our lunch. Dinner included rotten melon, and tough veal and so far Morocco's food seems to leave a lot to be desired. At any rate it didn't matter because we were all thoroughly exhausted and couldn't wait to go to bed.

Monday, October 4th

We awakened to good weather and had a nice breakfast on our terrace. The croissant was tasty and the apricot jam was fine.

After sleeping well we were eagerly looking forward to the days activities. Unfortunately we found out that Lila Suna was afflicted with a very sore, swollen and apparently infected arm, that will certainly handicap her on this trip. At any rate we took our tour bus to the Bahia Palace and the Jewish quarter. This took us into a terrible area with great poverty and sad eyed children, terrible biting flies abounded and there were awful shops somewhat like the ones we saw on the Via Dolorosa in Israel. The sight was almost as bad as when we first entered the square upon our arrival in Marrakech and saw the snake charmers, a poor little 5 year old girl dancing for money, monkeys frolicking and acrobats performing. The worst of it was the fact that you had to pay these people in order to take their pictures.

Luckily our lunch included good stewed peaches and then after sitting around the pool for a whole, we again got on our bus to visit a rug factory that was a complete rip off and the place smelled to high heaven. They served us tea and compelled us to stay there until they completed their spiel about rug making. But of course no one bought anything.

Then the bus driver took us to a brass and leather shop which was also a rip off, but thankfully we finally went off on our own and found some lovely shops in the new city where Al was able to buy a beautiful leather jacket, a Fendi suitcase, and a Cartier makeup kit for me. This was a great store, it had wonderful prices and was a far cry from the terrible shops to which our driver had taken us.

We decided we would not join the group for dinner but preferred being by ourselves and our choice was a good one. A nice little French restaurant called "Gôut Va Bien" where we had steak poivre and sweet melon. This was a very charming place with a little balcony on which we ate.

The taxi driver kindly waited for us and actually escorted us there from another restaurant where an English couple we saw advised us to leave as they said the food was terrible. It was a good thing that we heeded their advice.

After dinner we returned to the hotel only to find that several of our group had developed stomach problems. Al has a cold as well, so we went to bed early.

Tuesday, October 5th

Early in the morning we went to The Atlas Mountains on our bus. We drove through beautiful red winding roads and throughout the countryside the earth was a deep terracotta. The view was most impressive and we passed many interesting places including a Berber village where we stopped to shop. While there I bought some little ceramics, a statue and a small rock that seemed to have ancient writings on it. I was so excited when I saw it thinking it might be valuable. However I soon figured out that the stone had been painted to look real—what a con! These people were certainly crafty. They also loved to bargain. It was absolutely crazy the way they haggled with prospective customers.

At any rate we continued on our bus ride through little winding roads surrounded by rippling brooks and viewing the colorfully attired people in the area.

Our lunch was at a charming French inn on top of a mountain. The inn had an empty pool in the back and happily the day was beautiful with clear and crisp air and a true blue cloudless sky, which made the omelet we had, seem to be delicious. Maybe it really was anyway.

On the way back to the hotel after lunch the same vendors (the crafty ones) kept following us from stop to stop, lowering the prices wherever we stopped. It was quite amusing. They were on fast mopeds so they were always at these stops before we arrived.

In the PM we went back to the store where Al bought his leather jacket and Larry bought the same one as well as the bag we bought, so I guess the two men will start looking like twins.

Our dinner was at a charming Italian restaurant called "Trattoria". It was quite good and we sat on very comfortable Moorish banquettes. I had risotto, melon and stracciatteli soup. Our entire group was eating there too. (Naturally we all seemed to find the best places.)

Wednesday, October 6th—On to Rabat

Al woke up with a bad stomach so we did not think we could go to Rabat. However he took some kind of a pill and we hoped for the best. Therefore we decided to join the group and leave. We drove through a Berber marketplace that was most interesting, but filthy and crowded with raggedy people. There was a water bearer who was wearing several brass cups and a funny hat and many of the other townspeople were wearing caftans, and jalabas. It was an extremely colorful scene and presumably typical of the area.

We then proceeded onwards to Casablanca which was totally different. As we drove through the city we were able to see that it was a large, busy and thriving place with all white houses and buildings. We noticed the truly magnificent residential streets with houses that were gorgeous and enormous, and they looked much like the houses in California or Palm Beach. There were lovely flowers and huge hedges with pink hibiscus as well as geraniums and Bougainvillea and everything was lovely indeed.

We also saw many school girls in white smocks apparently enroute to school or an outing.

Lunchtime was upon us and we all went to a little French bistro where we ate outside on the beach. It was terrible, awful, and just plain bad food. Again there were the usual vendors who always seemed to follow us. This time they sold us copies of Cartier wallets right at the tables, while we ate. The wallets and other items were most attractive and the vendors enjoyed bargaining crazily and continuously. No doubt this is the usual way of conducting business in Morocco. (Thank heavens Al is apparently much better.)

Finally about 4:30PM we reached Rabat and checked in at the very large Hilton Hotel and it was lovely with beautiful gardens. We were given a nice room with attractive furnishings and after resting a while we went to dinner at a wonderful restaurant called "Chez Martenets" where I had the best rack of lamb I ever ate. It was extremely tender and delicate and Al also had the greatest tart tatin.

First we all sat at the bar on Moorish banquettes which were covered with a dark orange wool cloth. Then we were taken to our dining tables which were scattered haphazardly all around the room.

The host was a charming gentleman who spoke English very well and gave us what he termed "a cadeau" that was lobster mashed with another fish and covered with cognac, spices and gelatin on top and it was quite delish!

Thursday, October 7th

This morning we took a bus tour to the tomb of the present King Hussein the second's father. It was gorgeous, all tile and marble with a constant Koran reader sitting in the corner. They change the shifts of the readers every 2 hours, and I guess all through the night as well.

Also there were huge beautiful brass objects on the stairs outside and it was a most impressive sight.

Then we went to the Roman ruins where the gardens were filled with poisonous trumpet flowers and some gorgeous white and red blossoms that drooped down gracefully.

Next we went to the casbah (fortress) and the present King's home which is the palace, and we all took pictures with the guard at the gate, as he was extremely friendly. The Palace itself was quite long and had a green roof indicating a spiritual effect, and it also displayed a red flag with a green dot in the center. The red was to indicate the blood of the nation.

We then had lunch at Dar Es Alam the local golf course, which had beautiful flowers and shrubs all around, plus black and beige knoll chairs that were scattered all over. In the bar there was a fireplace and also round corners with stools fitting under very snugly. It was all extremely attractive.

We had been informed that the golf course was very good so Al played with Si Deutch while I played bridge with Phyllis, Esther Feldman and Roz Deutch.

And then an unusual event occurred. It seems that when Al and Si reached the 10th hole the starter came out and asked if they would mind letting the King's doctor play through. Graciously Al and Si agreed and then they both watched the doctor start to tee off. As he was ready to hit Al threw him a new golf ball and said "here's a nice American ball". The doctor was impressed and said "why don't you join me". The men said yes and when they reached the 18th hole Al invited the Dr. to have a drink with him. This became a period of great camaraderie and the doctor said if he was able to contact his wife he would like to invite Al and me for a couscous dinner at his home. Al explained that we were with a few other couples but the doctor said that would not matter and just to let him know how many people we would be.

So we invited the Goodmans and Cedars to join us and when the doctor called us to say his wife was agreeable, he then said he would pick up Al and myself in his car and would send a taxi to pick up the Cedars and the Goodmans.

Promptly at 7 PM Dr. Absalem Tazi who was a charming and attractive man called for us and told us he wanted people from other nations to see a Moroccan home and therefore was so anxious to invite us.

At any rate we got to his huge house behind a lovely iron gate that opened automatically and we were ushered into the square foyer approximately 16 x16, where his wife Anne graciously welcomed us. She was most attractive and was wearing a lovely French printed black dress and quite a large 2 strand pearl necklace.

The foyer had a burnt orange wallpaper with a blue print that seemed to be from Clarence House and there were also 3 Louis 16th sofas against the walls.

The living room was approximately 25 x 45 with banquettes, sofas, a fireplace, brass lamps, a mirrored coffee table, and several armless chairs.

Anne was really adorable. She had a good sense of humor and was definitely on the ball. Actually she was also a doctor and had met her husband in Paris where she had studied medicine.

We had brought them some wine as a gift because as Muslims they were not allowed to consume hard liquor. At any rate we remained in the living room for about half an hour just getting acquainted and where they served little plates of nuts and olives.

Then we went to the adjoining dining room for dinner. This was also a very large room with no center dining table. There were flowered banquettes all around the walls and just a small table at one side with eight little chairs around it. The table was covered with a crosstich table cloth which Anne said did not show the stitches on the wrong side. Also it was covered with a plastic top so that it would not get soiled. No doubt someone special had made it and it was treated with great care.

The dinner was terrific. First we had soup with tiny meat balls and lemon slices, and then we had bigger meat balls with carrots and potatoes.

After that the maid (who had 8 children and whose husband had 36 wives) brought in a tray of wine in tiny cups which she inadvertently spilled all over the carpeting and on Phyllis's white pants as well.

Anne promptly took Phyllis into her bedroom and dressed her in a magnificent and expensive pink satin caftan embroidered with a soutache and jeweled border that embellished the entire outfit. Phyllis looked beautiful in it and told Anne she would have it cleaned before she returned it. Anne then replied that in Morocco a person could not return a gift therefore Phyllis was now the new owner of the caftan. Incidentally Anne had the maid clean the carpeting with white wine which apparently takes out red wine stains.

Our next course after the spillage episode was "couscous" the most famous Moroccan dish. This was a huge tower of thin rice which contained lamb, onions, carrots, turnips, greens, coriander, cumin and pepper. The entire dish was delicious.

Then we were served a tray of grapes (both green and blue) with sections of pomegranate all over the tray. In Morocco it is possible to eat the pomegranate seeds as they are very soft and the actual fruit is white in color. Our entire dinner was a delicious treat and we truly enjoyed the company of our gracious guests.

However in the course of conversation Audrey mentioned something about her Rabbi which produced a lull in the conversation as the Tazi's did not know we were all Jewish.

At one point Dr. Tazi had mentioned that his daughter intended to go to America that Autumn to get her medical degree and Al said we would contact her and generally take her under our wing for which the Tazis were seemingly very grateful. Nevertheless after Audrey's statement about her Rabbi it no longer appeared that the girl would call us.

Dr. Tazi then drove us back to our hotel and despite the fact that Al wrote him a beautiful letter when we returned home, there was never a response to the letter nor did we ever again hear from any member of the Tazi family. It was too bad that our religion became such a no no.

Friday, October 8th

After a lovely breakfast on the terrace we took a bus ride through the town. We entered the Medina (the old town) and found ourselves in a 9th century world of commerce. There were little boutiques with thousands of people milling about and selling their wares. The dirty little alleyways were narrow and winding and there were many donkeys laden with baskets and boxes, including one with a TV on his back.

We then saw many little children polishing brass in the brass shops, fruit vendors with beautiful varieties of dry as well as fresh fruit products, and other vendors who displayed vegetables, clothing, belts, shoes and leather goods, etc. I must say it was an incredible sight to behold!

There were also people walking about shoulder to shoulder in both directions, some were tourists like us but others were native Moroccans.

We also visited courtyards of mosques and there was a wool area with a terrible stench which emanated from hanging sheepskins, plus children who urinated against the wall, and we then saw adorable little tots who were singing in the nearby Koran school.

Among the other existing items there were many pieces of meat hanging from doorways, paintings by local artists which were casually placed against the walls, and also a baby with a blue shaven head because of a bug affliction, who was haphazardly lying on the ground. Then too there were huge vats cooking unappetizing types of strange foods, and a myriad of brass shops abounded, all of which made the place seem like a bazaar unequaled in the entire world.

We then walked for 3 hours and witnessed hundreds of merchants and people in general simply marching around the area.

Finally after making many purchases of sundry odds and ends, we emerged from the Medina and arrived at a little bridge with the river running under it. Naturally we concluded that this whole episode was a wonderful experience that epitomized life as it existed in a distant past era, and still survived in the present time.

For lunch we had a great cheese, onion and tomato omelet and melon with Lenore Howard and Honey and Harold Cook, and then walked through the hotel gardens which was beautifully terraced and had tiled areas that continued down many flights of stairs to the lobby.

Afterwards Phyllis and I bought some brightly colored and attractive string bags outside the hotel from some friendly boys with whom we spent time chatting. They were very nice and were lots of fun so we had a good time.

Tea Time then arrived and Al and I spent it with Jerry Lazarowitz and Jackie his girl friend, at which time he told us a sad tale about his wife. Not everyone has a happy life as we all know too well.

Saturday, October 9th—Fez

Thankfully our room here was really lovely. It was all blue and white and nicely put together. The hotel was also beautiful even though it was quite ornate; however it was exceedingly comfortable and was hopefully going to make this trip quite pleasurable. The city Fez so far seemed to be quite interesting as well.

That evening we had dinner with a lovely Jewish couple Jack and Danielle who owned the boutique situated in the hotel lobby and they told us some intriguing things about Fez. It seemed that there were only 700 Jewish people left in the city whereas there used to be 20,000. In addition they said they themselves would have to leave when the present King dies as the new king to be, did not like the Jews. Also their children, who now went to a French school, would probably have to go to school in Paris where they intended to move. The other possibility for them would be to relocate in Israel. We enjoyed being with them as they were charming, and intelligent. They also invited us to their home for dinner but unfortunately we anticipated leaving Fez before that would be possible.

Sunday, October 10th

Our bus departed Fez for Mohamedia and en route we stopped for a pit stop at a dreadful little inn where the only available bathroom facility was a hole in the ground. It was smelly, wet and completely uncomfortable, plus it sorely needed information as to how a person was supposed to straddle the hole. The entire incident was terrible.

Nevertheless we continued on to the Hotel Meridian which was very nice. It had lots of colorful striped banquettes in the lobby with funny chairs shaped like flowers.

Then we walked to the pool area and saw several topless girls, a very strange sight as Morocco was thought to be more conservative, but maybe bosoms were not considered to be off limits there. One girl was also smoking a cigar! (She too was topless).

Lunch was most unsatisfactory. In fact it was awful. We just had shrimp, that cost an expensive $45 for two people.

After lunch we took a lovely walk to the golf course club house which was very plain although the course itself seemed nice.

Our dinner was in the hotel dining room where the ceiling was burgundy silk with brass piping on different levels. It was quite modern and attractive but the food was not good. (At least we would not gain weight).

We then went to bed early and Al was supposed to wake me at 5AM as we had to be on the bus early the next morning. Instead he woke me thinking it was already 6 AM so I rushed into the shower and dressed madly. He dashed downstairs to hold the bus only to find that it was 1 AM. We were hysterical laughing and then I had to undress and go back to bed. (Funny things do happen sometimes on these trips).

Monday, October 11th—Monte Carlo

We finally got up it 5 AM and were the first ones to board the bus on the way to the Casablanca airport for our trip to Nice.

First we had to make an unauthorized stop at Marseilles but ultimately arrived at Nice where the whole group took a bus to the Monte Carlo hotel, a huge place and commercial, but it had nice rooms.

We had our dinner at the Rampoldi and had very good vegetable soup, wonderful fish bonne femme with mushrooms plus delicious pineapple for dessert.

A lady at the next table who was wearing gorgeous large ruby drop earrings kindly gave us the names of several good local restaurants. She was a gracious French lady who actually lived in Monte Carlo so we presumed she knew the best places.

Tuesday, October 12th—Monte Carlo

I went to St. Laurent early this AM right after I left the hair dresser and was able to buy several things for Nancy and myself and I must say their clothing was outstanding.

Al and I were then just in time for lunch at the Hotel De Paris roof with the Goodmans and we had a delicious salad and tarte tatin which is my absolute favorite dessert. The roof was a truly beautiful place and Nettie Pollack my good friend from Quebec always told me that it was her first choice for the best restaurant on the Rivera.

After lunch we walked along the Avenue de Moulins (the nice shopping street) and there we met our whole tour in Dana Côte D'Azur where everything was lovely and priced well.

Dinner was at Le Bec Rouge and unfortunately this time it was not so good. I had feuillitté de Morelles that was okay but the duck that Al had was bad, bad, bad. The desserts looked awful and we didn't order any of them, so we then returned to the Hotel. Sad to say Al does not feel well.

Wednesday, October 13th

We had our usual breakfast in the room and then picked up the Goodmans and were all off to Nice. Again we spent some time at St. Laurent where this time I was able to buy some lovely pants and a blouse for Nancy and I was sure she would love everything I bought.

All the stores closed at noon so we hardly had any time to shop and therefore it became an early lunch hour. Of course St. Moritz was the choice and as always lunch was delicious. Cheese soufflé and tart tatin was everybody's selection and we enjoyed ourselves thoroughly until they told us some very sad news. This was about our friends the Bousidans.

We were terribly upset when we were told that Armand Bousidan was hit by a taxi in front of the Negresco 3 years ago and died instantly. He was one of the loveliest men we ever knew and we were really devastated.

There was also a friend of Audrey's in the restaurant and a little time was spent chatting with her, then after that we drove back to Monte Carlo.

Al was still not feeling well and we were really quite worried. He had fever for 2 days and we thought it might be a kidney attack.

At any rate we had a light dinner, in the hotel coffee shop with the Cedars and Sunas, where we just had onion soup and salad and then went to bed early, although we did make a stop at La Reserve first to see if Shirley and Eddie had arrived as we were supposed to have dinner with them the next night. The hotel was still gorgeous but the Rothensteins were not expected until tomorrow. I certainly hope we can keep the date if Al is well enough.

Thursday, October 14th

Calamity struck! We had to call a doctor (a lady) for Al at 3 AM. He had fever and chills and we were both extremely concerned. We wondered whether we'd be able to stay with the group and return to New York with them on Saturday or if we would have to leave by ourselves immediately.

After the doctor left however he did seem to feel a little better so I went to San Remo with the Goodmans. The town was extremely busy with all the crazy Italians driving every which way and we were unable to find the stores we wanted so Audrey kept yelling out the Window "Fendi, Gucci, Fendi, Pucci, and finally a knowledgeable Italian understood her and directed us to the proper street.

Luckily we were able to park in the same spot we had last time we went there and then went to the Chanel Shop, Enrico Cremieux (the best shop) and Ferragamo's etc. where we really outdid ourselves shopping like mad. Everything was beautiful with excellent prices so we had a terrific time and we went back to Monte Carlo laden with bundles.

Audrey and I then went to Rompaldi for lunch where we had great onion soup and then marched around Monte Carlo for a short time. Al was not so good but not too bad.

Friday, October 15th

During the night Al again was quite ill so we had to call Sidney Rothstein twice in America. We finally reached him and as we suspected he diagnosed Al as having a urinary tract infection. He gave us the French equivalent name of the proper medication he needed which I was able to obtain at a local chemist. The lady doctor here was absolutely incapable but after taking the pills Sidney prescribed Al felt much better and we hoped to be able to go home tomorrow, however Sidney thought we should stay and return Sunday with the group.

Saturday, October 16th

Shirley and Eddie came to visit us and we entertained them on our terrace with Al looking dapper in just underpants. We had fun with them but of course we did not go out to dinner.

Sunday, October 17th

Thank goodness we were able to leave Monte Carlo for New York. Al was much better and we hoped to get home in one piece. Farewell Monte Carlo and once again Au Revoir!

Saturday, October 29th, 1983—Leave For Tokyo

We met Nancy and Jeff at the airport and first went to the Clipper Club Lounge to meet the Phil Waterman's and Jackie and Ronnie Rofay.

We ultimately boarded the plane and were sitting upstairs in 1st class which was extremely comfy but there was no movie.

We also had a lovely lunch, caviar (my absolute favorite), salad, roast beef, vegetable and a nice dessert.

The trip was uneventful although we had ice cream with chocolate sauce for a snack, and then fruit cup and Nova Scotia on pumpernickel for a luncheon repast.

After 14 ½ hours we arrived at the Tokyo airport to find our luggage waiting for us, all stacked up together. Nancy's and Jeff's luggage were already in a cart.

Our man from the hotel was already there with a welcome sign and then he drove us for another hour and a half to the hotel. It was a pleasant drive although it was now dusk.

The hotel was enormous and we had a very nice room where a beautiful bouquet of roses and orchids had already arrived from American Express with a welcoming note. This was certainly a kind gesture.

In the morning we arose to witness the blush of dawn. There was a rosy glow over the entire horizon and then a big red sunrise appeared. This was truly "the land of the rising sun".

An added feature were the wonderful amenities in our room. There were slippers and beautiful robes for both of us. A little stool was in the bathroom where the top lifted so that soiled towels could be placed inside. The light apparatus was conveniently placed so that you hardly had to move your arm in the dark to turn it on and everything else in the room was most accessible. I must say the Japanese were really ingenious and thought only of the comfort of their guests.

We had breakfast in the Camellia room downstairs, juice, croissants and tea and everything was delicious.

Nancy and Jeff were already waiting for us when we got to the car. The driver was ready too and we all went to the Meijes shrine which had beautiful park like surroundings.

There were lots of adorable school children ages 4 to 8 dressed in little red caps and blue jackets and they were picking up nuts and going to see the ceremony with a group of young Buddhists who were on their way to worship. The Buddhists were dressed in white with black heavy clogs and were also wearing shiny fur like hats. They were all marching in a line to the shrine where many visitors were seated, waiting to hear the prayers.

Then we went to the lake where the Chrysanthemum display and Bonsai exhibit took place. The mums were lovely and one plant had two hundred blossoms all separately tied. There were also beautiful fish swimming on the lake, plus a tea house and lovely walks were nearby.

After that we drove past the Imperial Palace but could not enter it as it was not open at that hour. However we did see the lovely Fir trees surrounding a moat with the Palace beyond it.

Next was the "Ginza" a busy thoroughfare like 5th Avenue and we entered a department store where I bought a crazy sweater. It was quite like one I had seen in New York for so much more money.

Finally we returned to the hotel for lunch which we had in the Japanese room and then the problem started.

We all thought we would be ordering carefully, as Al was extremely allergic to Sesame and therefore when he ordered a crab meat dish, we had no idea it could be devastating. However it was accompanied by a harmless looking sauce, so when he dipped the crabmeat into it, none of us had any indication that it was made with Sesame.

However all of a sudden Al realized he was having a reaction and immediately passed out just like he did at the Verby wedding and at the Woodmere Club one night. It was terrible as he turned blue and became icy and then threw up.

Luckily the restaurant brought in a doctor immediately and they put a screen around our table, got Al into a wheel chair, and then took him through the kitchen and up the back way to our room. The door was already open, the bed was turned down and a nurse was there in attendance. I never saw such amazing precision care for a person in distress. I don't think the best hospital in America could compete with this wonderfully coordinated episode.

Al of course who had just gone through an anaphylactic shock event was able to sleep it off for the entire afternoon, but of course none of us were able to see much of Tokyo after that.

That night Nancy and Jeff had dinner with some business people and Al and I ate in the coffee shop. I had shrimp pilaf and some melon and Al just had tea and toast.

Thank heavens he felt better but it certainly was an upsetting situation and we were deeply concerned about the rest of this trip food wise.

Tuesday, November 1st

We again had breakfast in the Camellia room with good eggs, tangerines and croissants and thank heavens Al seemed okay.

After that we were able to have the car and driver again in order to go shopping, but first Jeff had an omelet with ham and cheese and they put a little square of each on top of the omelet. It really looked very cute.

So then we all returned to the Ginza and tried to shop but really were not enthusiastic about anything in particular.

Then we went to the Imperial Hotel at the Brasserie for lunch as we were worried about Al's eating any place else. He was able to have a niçoise salad which was quite good and the place was delightful and true to the period of the Belle époque.

A visit to the Hanae Mori shop proved to be a success as I bought a beautiful blouse. However when I returned to the hotel I noticed that it was stained on the sleeve. Nevertheless when I called to tell them, they promised to send me another blouse in the morning before we left for Hong Kong.

They kept their promise and I did receive another blouse which was a wee bit larger but certainly better than having a dirty one.

We had a lovely dinner on the hotel roof with one of Jeff's cohorts who lived in Tokyo and where I had rack of lamb prepared beautifully and everything else was great.

Wednesday, November 2nd

So off we were to Hong Kong after a very nice flight, but when we got to the airport we found it to be dirty, filthy and completely unlike Tokyo which was so orderly and clean. This place was hot and looked like an opium den.

After a lengthy wait we finally got our luggage and a black Rolls Royce picked us up to go to our Hotel Mandarin.

The city was all lit up when we arrived and was very colorful. The hotel was beautiful but it was located in a business section near Jeff's office. He went directly to the office so I guess it was a worthwhile vicinity for him. Al and I however went right to bed as the trip to Hong Kong had been wearying.

Thursday, November 3rd—Hong Kong

The coffee shop in the hotel was very nice and we had a lovely breakfast and the tea holder was exceptionally attractive. In fact I wanted to buy it but they would not sell it to me.

Then Nancy called and took us to a tailor for AL to get some suits and also to a shirt maker for him. Apparently everybody who comes to Hong Kong has to return home laden with new clothing. I guess my turn was next.

We went to a dim sum restaurant for lunch called the "Blue Heaven" with Jeff's office people. They had little wagons there which they wheeled around and which were laden with different foods. All of them were terrible.

You could actually grab what you wanted from the carts if you could possibly find something edible. (I personally did not).

The place was enormous and had a noise level beyond the charts but I thought I was going to be forced to become a member of Jenny Craig or Weight Watchers out of necessity. (The reason being, AWFUL FOOD!)

Oh for the good old days and the 35 cents Chinese lunch in New York including soup and dessert, all of which was delish!

After lunch we went to the C.A.C. (the Chinese art building). It contained a load of Hong Kong junk but was great fun to see it. We took the subway there which I did not like so we took the ferry back and that was very nice.

We had our dinner at the Shanghai Friendship Club with some of Jeff's people and it was an all Shanghai crab dinner. This was awful and disgusting food but lovely people. I must say I was impressed with Jeff as he ate about 40 crabs and seemed to enjoy them all.

Jackie and Ronnie Rafé were with us for dinner and they were really nice as they usually are, plus Menola the Head of the Office and Vicki, she was the daughter of the Philippine Ambassador to Spain and was very pretty. He was a Count. Frank the host was a top broker and his wife Lucia was also lovely. There was Nancy who worked in the office and Dorothy another broker. They were all Chinese except for the Watermans who were there as well.

Dessert was a pumpkin that had rice and fruit in it. This was awful too and the sad story was that I could not possibly eat this food.

Happily we met the Klombergs and Katz's for tea at the Mandarin that evening and it was really wonderful seeing them so far from home.

Friday, November 4th

This day we were on our own. Nancy dumped us and I didn't blame her as we really did not like to eat the same things she and Jeff did so it was better that we stayed with more American food, while they could experiment with the Asian stuff, therefore Al and I wandered around alone and had a great time doing and seeing what we wished all day.

We had dinner at Jimmy's Kitchen and enjoyed it tremendously, especially the dessert which was deep fried ice cream with chocolate sauce. It was yum yum indeed.

Saturday, November 5th

Today we went to Kowloon and wandered around the Hotel Peninsula and had lunch there with Sol and Muriel Kaplan from the Woodmere Club whom we bumped into unexpectedly. We also visited one of Al's jewelers.

In the afternoon I bought a few blouses at the Peninsula and then we returned on the ferry to our side of the city where we went to the bead store and I must say I had a really terrific time. I bought lots of beads to string back home, coral, ivory and jade, etc and I intended designing my own necklaces.

Then we met Nancy and Jeff for dinner at the Chinese restaurant at the Mandarin Hotel. Again the food was AWWWFULLL!

Sunday November 6th

What a great day! We went to the Stanley Market which was a shopping Medina and loads of fun.

While there we bought several black market polo shirts, and actually found them when Nancy went in a little shop and tapped her finger on her chest where the insignia should have been, so the sales person understood her and took us into the back of the store where he had hidden the phony polos.

There were many narrow little winding streets there, it was extremely crowded with lots of people shopping for Bargains, and it was reminiscent of Morocco. There were also some beautiful new apartment houses a block or so away from the market which appeared to be expensive. Then we also drove past the Ocean City Peak that had a sea horse dug out in the mountain. The terrain was quite hilly and bumpy as well.

By the way the apartment houses that we saw were cut into levels on the hills and really were incredible.

Our last stop was Hollywood Road a famous street in Hong Kong. It was filled with lovely antiques and was most pleasurable. They particularly had old jade in many colors; lavender, green and white etc. The lavender pieces were really gorgeous and the road itself was bustling with shoppers and most of them were busy making purchases.

That night Al and I had dinner at the Mandarin with Nancy, Jackie and Jane as Jeff had to go to Singapore. A famous French chef was doing the cooking (Louis Onthier from Cannes at the La Napoulé). It was quite good for a change, so we actually had a great dinner American style.

Monday, November 7th

That morning we took a cab to Aberdeen and saw the junks, the boat people and the little village. The junks were very colorful, mostly red, and the people on them were quite raggedy and poor in appearance. After that we went to another poor area, the Cat and Ladder street near Hollywood Road which was fascinating to see. Our next stop was to the various shops in Kowloon where we had a buffet lunch on the veranda of the Peninsula Hotel. Everything there was lovely and beautiful.

Then after lunch I met Lavana Hirschberg, (Moshe's sister from Israel) and she kindly took me to a wonderful little wholesale place to buy magnificent table cloths for Barbi. They were all hand embroidered on linen and organdy and were fairly inexpensive. I know in America the same type would have been about $2000 a cloth whereas I didn't pay more than $200 each.

After that we had dinner with her at the Jewish Club where they were planning a fashion show which was really like a Hadassah meeting in the five towns. Finally she took us to see her temple and to see her apartment. Her husband was the chief Rabbi in Hong Kong so they knew most of the Jewish people there. Then after dinner they took us to Victoria Peak which was quite a distance away but they wanted us to see Jumbo which had 3 restaurants on the water and was all lit up. It was an unbelievable sight and we were so happy to have seen it.

Tuesday, November 8th

Finally we were through viewing all the landmarks of this city and are now homebound—just in time for Kenny's birthday and elated to have been on this wonderful trip. Thank you Nancy and Jeff.

Bye Bye Hong Kong

Conclusion

This travel diary has now come to its final page, as the next many trips I took were mainly repeated visits. In other words I once again returned to the same special places I loved, and therefore the exuberance I had experienced when first arriving at a new country just didn't exist.

I really loved repeating my returns to these now "well known" spots but to reiterate my activities in diary form would serve no purpose and might be boring to any possible readers. It certainly did not warrant any additional writing.

So until that hopeful "some day" when I arrive at an uncharted area, this volume will have to suffice, and therefore I now must say Adieu, Ciao, Shalom, Hasta La Vista, Sayonara, etc.

Addendum

The memories of past events are precious and thank heavens I'm able to recall so many of mine.